NOT REALLY WHAT YOU'D CALL A WAR

La Moqueuse taken by a French war photographer
(Commandant Moreau centre left)

NOT REALLY WHAT YOU'D CALL A WAR

Norman Hampson

Whittles Publishing

Typeset by
Whittles Publishing Services

Published by
Whittles Publishing,
Roseleigh House,
Latheronwheel,
Caithness, KW5 6DW,
Scotland, UK

ISBN 1-870325-38-9

Printed by Interprint Ltd., Malta

CONTENTS

to the ship's company of La Moqueuse

PREFACE

The first thing that I ought to say about this book is that its existence involves the breaking of a promise. As far back as 1944 I vowed to earn not merely the admiration but the gratitude of posterity by being the only RNVR officer not to write a book about his experiences. Since I was on what was known as 'active' service for four years and in contact with the enemy for about fourteen days, it did not look as though posterity was going to miss very much. A lifetime's experience as a historian has led me to change my mind. Battles are rather out of fashion and since there has been something of a vogue for 'history from below', I thought there might be a case for something that begins as 'history from below decks' and shows what it felt like to be swept up in a communal experience that must seem to the present generation almost as remote as the days of Hornblower. The not-so-gentle reader, in pursuit of blood and guts, is therefore advised to put this book back on the shelves before a friendly shop assistant asks if he or she can be of any assistance.

Like any self-respecting historian, I must establish my credentials by saying something about my sources. There are three of these: a diary of sorts, my letters home and my memory. The diary is essentially a record of where I was at any particular time; information which, until the spring of 1944, we were not allowed to reveal in letters home. It is accurate as far as it goes and it poses no problems of interpretation. Unfortunately it hardly goes anywhere at all, where my first three years of war service are concerned. From about the time of the allied landing in the south of France in August 1944 it provides a much fuller account of what I was doing and seeing and it has the advantage of being written as a record that was not designed to influence or reassure any particular audience.

My letters to my parents pose rather more problems. I usually wrote home two or three times a week and they kept all my letters. Over a period of almost four years that constitutes quite an archive and it is one to which no previous historian has had access! It is, unfortunately, a highly selective one, for in the first place there was the business of censorship and we were not allowed to say anything about where we were or what we were doing. When I was an ordinary seaman a casual reference to the fact that my ship, *Carnation*, was a corvette, resulted in a neat hole in my letter home. If the German Admiralty had got hold of this priceless information (which they were quite capable of working out for themselves), I doubt if it would have resulted in any significant change to their grand strategy. Someone I met had informed his girl friend that, when they opened the mess-deck portholes in the morning, 'a strange invisible perfume hits the wharves'. That was excised too. When, as an officer, I censored my own mail, I allowed myself an occasional reference to the beauty of the local scenery but on the whole I played by the rules. Anything really interesting, such as our share in the sinking of an Italian submarine or the fact that an ammunition ship had blown up within a quarter of a mile of us, was completely taboo. When I had enjoyed a particularly interesting leave, I evaded the geographical ban by substituting a shore address for the name of my ship. That could have got me into serious trouble. The letters themselves were inoffensive enough, but by putting one and one together, my parents could work out that *La Moqueuse*, with her twin 4" gun, was somewhere in the eastern Mediterranean. If the Germans had known *that*, they might have invaded Turkey or withdrawn from Italy while there was still time!

With all the more interesting subjects excluded, the problem was to think of anything that I *was* allowed to mention, once the family chat had been exhausted, I devoted innumerable pages to the implications of my ambitions to become a poet; my success or failure in getting my poems accepted by various periodicals and anthologies; and to my attempts to preserve a 'little magazine', *Phoenix*, that a friend and I had launched just before the war. Thanks to the efforts of my father, it staggered on until about 1944, when the mobilization of one editor after another proved too much for it. My poetical aspirations involved a veritable obsession with the verse and philosophy of Keats, as mediated by John Middleton Murry. This provoked much speculation about the significance of my experience and my attitude towards participation in the war. I have included a few brief references to these cogitations when they seem to typify problems faced by people of my generation and I have also included a few of my poems, to serve as contemporary documents. I will, however, spare the reader my protracted comments on the strategy of the Red Army, which I relied on to bring the war to a victorious conclusion 'within a year' (September, 1941) 'before long' (December 1941), 'this winter' (November 1942 and again in July 1943), 'by the end of the year' (April 1944), 'by Armistice Day' (August 1944) and 'within six months' (November 1944). Well, I got it right in the end. It did seem relevant, however, to summarize the evolution of my attitudes towards the nature of the war and the prospects for an enduring peace since my confused idealism and naivety were probably typical of many of my contemporaries.

I was also devoured by a passion for all things historical, whose intensity increased in proportion to the square of their age. While I was still in England I would walk miles to see and sketch an Early English arch in some ruined church, and as for the pyramids and Luxor... It was my good fortune (if not that of my long-suffering parents) to spend two and a half years operating in the vicinity of some of the most spectacular sights in the Mediterranean world. Sea-going folk rarely had access to the transport that would have allowed them to exploit such opportunities, but from time to time one could take a few days' leave. This gave me a chance to re-live my travels by describing them in letters home, building by building and almost stone by stone – the summary of my trip to Cairo and Luxor ran to 37 typewritten pages. Since almost all of this information can be found, rather more accurately, in any contemporary guidebook, I have included only the odd experience that is unlikely to happen to the present-day tourist, such as entering Damascus on a travelling crane and exploring Thebes on donkey-back.

My correspondence was also subject to self-censorship of a somewhat personal kind. I was supposed to be teetotal and to abstain from lewd company where they used words like 'damn' and 'bloody'. This meant that a certain amount of my naval experience had to be edited. I suppressed any references to our infrequent brushes with the official Enemy but I took the view that my daily encounters with my commanding officer fell outside the Official Secrets Act. Even here, however, I did not want to commit the wartime offence of spreading 'alarm and despondency' and I tried to conceal the extent to which I had more urgent problems than those posed by the Axis Powers.

My voluminous correspondence, in other words, leaves out a good deal that my parents would have liked to know and includes much that my present readers would not. Nevertheless, it has its value as well as its limitations. If I claimed to have seen something, it probably happened. If I expressed approval or indignation, that was how I felt at the time. In a way, it resembles my diaries: when the appropriate allowances have been made, it can be relied on as far as it goes.

That leaves memory as my final source – and historians are inclined to be scathing about the reliability of *that*. They may go too far. on re-reading my first two sources I have been agreeably surprised to discover how closely they correspond to what I think that I remember, give or take a little rearrangement to enhance the dramatic effect. In one or two cases I may be inclined to confuse what I saw for myself with what I heard at the time. I *think* I can recall seeing a commando group operating from a commandeered yacht that was flying the Jolly Roger, but I would not like to swear to it in a court of law. On the whole though, I am inclined to trust my memory on matters of fact.

What I thought about them at the time is a different matter. Up to a point, my attempt to rediscover N. Hampson is the sort of problem faced by any historian when he tries, on the basis of people's recollected impressions, to project himself into a character, but things are rather different when that character was me. I should like to think that I have more privileged access to N. Hampson than to Napoleon Bonaparte, and yet … I may know that when N. Hampson wrote something or other, he was suppressing part of the facts or his feelings – or I may now think that I can remember that he behaved then as I would behave now. How can

I be sure that we are dealing with the same person? The premises have not changed and the firm still trades under the same title, but I cannot be certain that I react now as I did then to what both past and present management agree to have happened. When I think that I am remembering how I felt, I may be merely attributing to my old self the kind of reactions that my present one would consider appropriate. Since I do not know how to navigate such treacherous waters, whenever possible I will stick to the 'facts' and concentrate on the events themselves.

That will only take us so far. Any autobiographical writing must aim at some sort of a balance between the private and the public, the inner and the outer man or woman. I suspect that concentration on the former is liable to be somewhat bogus, in the sense that the writer cannot avoid trying to sell the reader some sort of a persona that, for one reason or another, he believes to have constituted his 'real' self. I suspect that the inner man, in the present case, was a bit of a bore and I have certainly no intention of hanging out the constituent parts of his psyche in order to give them a good airing. What interests me, and I hope may entertain others, is the public side of things, the experiences that confronted me, like so many other people, as we passed from undergraduate to ordinary seaman and to commissioned officer. Things admittedly took a rather unusual turn in my own case, when I went on to become the British Naval Liaison Officer in a Free French ship. Apart from that, what happened to me was part of the collective experience of the war. This is primarily a 'Tale of Two Navies', the British and the Free French, together with a passing glimpse at the strange conditions prevailing in the south of France in the months that followed its liberation. If, in the course of my narrative, I give the impression of being rather less than enthusiastic about the Royal Navy as I experienced it, I must emphasize that I am talking about a period over fifty years ago and I expect that things are very different now.

CHAPTER 1

PREPARING FOR SEA

In June 1941 I was nineteen years old and I had just completed my first year as an undergraduate at Oxford when I volunteered for the navy. There was nothing in any way heroic about this decision since I was due to register for some kind of military service a couple of days later. All the same, it did constitute a choice, or, to be more precise, two choices. The first of these concerned the legitimacy of my taking part in a war, even in this war. Trying to reconstruct my state of mind at the time from my letters home, I think that I saw the war as a kind of international crusade against what I rather vaguely thought of as 'fascism'. That was something that had to be suppressed – I had been a vehement opponent of 'appeasement' – and it could only be eliminated by force. At the same time I regarded *all* forms of killing as morally indefensible. As I wrote to my parents soon after I was called up, 'I'm convinced that the Christian attitude, even to this war, is pacifism... But the consequences are so awful that I just can't face them.' I elaborated on this a couple of years later. 'If, in the twentieth century, we haven't got beyond the idea of justice, we had better give up. I believe I am wrong to fight ... hatred breeds hatred. I am fighting because I cannot humiliate myself to the position I should occupy if Nazism had not been opposed by force.' As I saw it at the time, my participation in the war was the product of cowardice rather than patriotism. Holding these somewhat contradictory views, I should either have declared myself a conscientious objector or volunteered for military service as soon as I was old enough. Instead I behaved rather like Auden's conventional citizen,

When there was peace, he was for peace;

When there was war, he went.

In other words, like all my friends, I allowed things to happen and waited on events.

Where I differed from them was in opting for the navy. This did indicate a positive choice. As an undergraduate, I had been doing a day's military training every week and I seem to remember that I had assumed that I would end up in the army,

1

like everyone else. I can think of several reasons that may have helped me to change my mind. Llike historians grappling with rather more serious problems, I can identify the causal factors involved, but I have no objective means of assessing their relative importance.

From the time when I was a small boy I had been fascinated by ships – and very apprehensive about sailing in any of them. I had the impression that the Germans were rather more efficient than the British when it came to land warfare, but that the situation was perhaps reversed at sea. If I was going to encounter any of them, it seemed a good idea to do so while playing our national game rather than theirs. I can also remember seeing a newsreel film in which a coastal convoy was being bombed, and feeling quite fiercely that this was something that ought not to be allowed to happen and that my place was 'out there', helping to protect the merchant ships. Convoy escort duty – which is what I was going to do for the rest of the war – was a non-belligerent sort of fighting where success consisted in avoiding contact with the enemy. That made it easier to fit into my somewhat self-contradictory views about participating in the war, since I could persuade myself that what I was doing was helping to deliver supplies to the civilian population. That was, at best, a convenient evasion, since we delivered military supplies as well and I participated in one or two assault convoys, but it probably helped. What may have turned the scales was an incident that occurred during my military training. One day I saw more advanced students practising bayonet fighting and being made to scream obscenties as they prodded their sandbags. This struck me as being just about as far as human degradation could go, and there seemed much to be said in favour of a more gentlemanly service in which people killed each other at several miles range, without actually seeing each other's faces. All of these factors probably influenced my decision, together with others that I have forgotten, or of which I was unaware. I was encouraged by my father, who had not formed a very favourable impression of the army during his service in the previous war. Where the navy was concerned, distance had lent enchantment to his view.

Young gentlemen – and anyone at Oxford could be regarded as a temporary acting gentleman – were allowed to volunteer for the navy as 'Commission Warrant' or CW ratings. In common parlance the initials were of course reversed. CW ratings served on the lower deck for a minimum of three months, as ordinary seamen, after which they went before a selection board. If successful, they then joined an officer training course. The first step was to pass a medical test. All that I can remember of mine is that, while chatting to the examining doctor, I managed to memorize the bottom line of the eye-chart, and even to repeat it backwards when he tested the other eye. This was probably an unnecessary precaution; at that time they were not being very fussy. A friend of mine, in a similar situation mistook for 'Are you fit?' an enquiry about whether or not he suffered from fits. His vigorous affirmative seemed to surprise the doctor but he still passed.

On June 10 I was due for interview, at a house in north Oxford, to decide whether or not I qualified for CW status. On the previous evening I went round to confirm the time of the interview. When no one answered the door I went to the back, where an elderly gardener was trundling a lawnmower. I chatted to him about his grass and he took me round to have another try at the front door. This time it was opened by a four-ringed captain, who addressed the gardener as 'sir'. When he had gone back to his lawnmowing I asked the captain who he was, and was told that he was the admiral who would preside over tomorrow's interview. It looked as though I was off to a good start.

I can't remember anything about the interview itself, except that I was asked to identify various kinds of warships, represented by models on the table. I could have done that when I was ten, but I can appreciate the board's problem. How does one decide whether or not a history student whose experience of ship-handling has been confined to punts, will make a good naval officer? I don''t suppose they turned many people down.

The circumstances of my induction into the navy gave me a foretaste of what was to come. On July 22 I received a rather fierce letter, which I was told that I was not allowed to challenge, instructing me that I should be required to report for duty in a year's time. Since I had been expecting something much more immediate, I felt no inclination to argue. A fortnight later, another letter ordered me to report to HMS *Collingwood* on August 19. When I duly presented myself at the training base, just outside Portsmouth, a puzzled officer told me that they were not expecting me until the following summer. Always ready to oblige, I offered to come back later, but he said that since I was already there I might as well stay. If he had decided the other way and played by the rules … I should never have met my wife. I have always been puzzled by the reluctance of historians to acknowledge the importance of chance.

My father, drawing on his experience of the Western Front, warned me that discipline during my initial training was likely to be harsh but that the atmosphere would improve when I joined a fighting unit. Forewarned by him, and by all the music hall jokes about sergeants, I prepared for the worst. What actually happened in *Collingwood* came as a pleasant surprise. The odd warrant officer tended to sneer and be on the look-out for such misdemeanours as he could provoke or invent, but almost all those in authority over us were understanding, reasonably patient and unmistakably fellow-members of the human race. Even the leading seamen who did their best to bark obscenities at us when they took us for arms drill, were making such an unconvincing attempt to play at sergeants that they were more amusing than intimidating.

Although HMS *Collingwood* was treated as a kind of honorary ship – on one's evenings off one went 'ashore' – it actually consisted of a large number of huts, each accommodating twenty-five trainees. These huts were grouped into 'divisions', named after the different parts of a ship's rigging … as these had existed in Nelson's time. We were in the foretop division. All this seemed rather remote from the world of submarines and dive-bombers. Most of the people in my hut came, like me, from the north. They included a contingent from the north-east whom I would have described as 'stroppy' if my naval vocabulary had been more advanced. I remember one man as being quite exceptionally awkward and cantankerous – until he got drunk. After that he became obsessed with not hurting other people's feelings, waking them up to make sure they realized that he was apologising to them for lurching up against their beds.

I was probably not as tactful as I might have been; one tends not to be, at nineteen. I remember one of the north-eastern contingent greeting with blank incomprehension my suggestion that, with all its undoubted merits, Middlesbrough was perhaps not the most beautiful of English towns. Of course, if you have never seen any other... After we had been 'on board' for a week, we were allowed out every other evening. Many of my new 'shipmates' made a beeline for the nearest tailor in Fareham, to get themselves measured for 'tiddley suits'. Since we had just been kitted out with two new uniforms apiece and we were paid at the princely rate of 2/6 (12½p) a day, I did not feel disposed to visit tailors – but they had other priorities and what came first was the urge to cut a dash with more plunging necklines and even wider bell-bottoms. They also spent uncomplaining hours scrubbing away at their collars in the hope of fading them into what was known as 'Mediterranean blue', which at least gave them a grudging respect for the quality of naval dye.

Naval uniforms were something else that went back to Nelson''s day and they were not very well adapted to twentieth-century life. The main problem was pockets. A tiny breast pocket was so contrived that as soon as you bent down everything fell out. Valuables were stored in a belt underneath the flap in the front of your trousers. If you wanted to get at them you looked as though you were about to expose yourself. We were supplied with warm and comfortable greatcoats, but putting them on over our uniforms looked like another offence against public decency. The problem was to get our collars to lie flat and the solution was for sailor A to stand just in front of sailor B, put his hands under B's armpits and hold his collar down while B put his coat on, after which the rôles were reversed. When we went around in public – without our greatcoats – young ladies would sometimes give our collars a surreptitious touch, in the hope that it would bring them luck. That didn't happen to the people in the army and the air force, but it was an inadequate compensation for all our sartorial disadvantages.

Each hut, although actually under the control of a petty officer, had a 'leader' drawn from the twenty-five recruits. As the only CW rating in our particular hut, that poisoned chalice was handed to me. When we were under instruction, I was merely one of the twenty-five. When it came to chores like cleaning our hut, I was supposed to allocate the jobs and supervise their execution, without doing any of them myself. That did not make for social harmony and the more obstreperous of my 'shipmates' complained to our petty officer that I was victimizing them. That was not very plausible since I had a much quieter life if I allocated the more unpopular jobs to the less strident members of the hut. I was semi-demoted and henceforth shared my command with another trainee. This gave me a quieter life, at the cost of exposing what I already suspected – that I was somewhat deficient in the vital power-of-command-and-officer-like-qualities that were supposed to go with commissioned status.

The man who determined whether our lives would be reasonably pleasant or a succession of little miseries was the petty officer in charge of our hut. We had the very good fortune to be entrusted to 'Wiggy' Bennet, an ancient mariner who might have come out of one of W.W. Jacobs' short stories. Wiggy had retired before the war (to judge by his appearance, rather a long time before it) and he took a somewhat relaxed view of his new responsibilities. I would describe his attitude as paternalist if he had not been a good deal less formidable than my own father in one of his reforming moods. In the most amiable way, Wiggy inducted us into a service whose traditions, habits and vocabulary had all become part of his identity.

Wiggy would not have been the man he was if he had not enlivened his instruction on this and that with yarns about things that had happened to him in far-off days. I remember one tale of how he stole a chicken from the captain's galley and took it up the mast to eat it in full view of the ship's company. His best story concerned an incident in Malta, when one of Wiggy's friends, who was shortly to appear amongst the first lieutenant's defaulters, came to him for advice, on the ground that Wiggy and No. 1 seemed to get on suspiciously well.

'Well, you see, 'im and me's Masons.'

'I thought there must be something like that. Haven't you got some sort of secret sign that you make to each other? If I gave 'im one it might put 'im in a good mood.'

'Oh I couldn't tell you anything about that. It's a secret.'

Eventually the good-natured Wiggy allowed himself to be persuaded. When encountering a Mason, a fellow-member of the fraternity sticks his thumbs into his ears and waggles his fingers as vigorously as possible. This his friend duly did, in front of the first lieutenant and the result was a defaulters' session that was not easily forgotten. This is one of those occasions when I have more confidence in the reliability of my memory than in the veracity of the information recalled, but it makes a good story.

I gather from my letters home that I was quite favourably impressed by the relevance of the training that we received, which allowed us to cope when we found ourselves at sea. Looking back on my own experience, I think that must have been true, and it is one of memory's little quirks that makes me recall things like sheerlegs and how to construct and operate them. Sheerlegs is, or are, a sort of Boy Scout improvisation consisting of three tree trunks lashed together to form a tripod, which can then be used as a crane. According to Wiggy, there was only one set of sheerlegs in existence in the entire British Empire and we would certainly never be allowed near it, but I suppose someone thought the information would come in useful if we ever found ourselves stranded on a desert island.

We were also put through a fair amount of what was known as 'field training', presumably to train us in instant obedience rather than to prepare us to come to the support of the army. I have a rather hazy recollection that we learned how to form fours and form two-deep, even though the practice had been abandoned. We certainly learned the complicated evolutions necessary in order to present arms with fixed bayonets when standing underneath an awning. Since the use of awnings had been discontinued for the duration of the war, this was certainly taking a long-term view of our likely period of service. After our preliminary training we moved on to gunnery. Very much to my surprise, I discovered that I seemed to have something of a natural aptitude for this, in the sense that I tended to do the right thing more or less instinctively. That scarcely corresponded to the way in which I thought of myself and I suspected – quite rightly – that when it came to the real thing I should be put off by the noise.

Eventually our ten weeks' training came to an end and we were shipped off by truck to our next destination. CW ratings were separated from the rest of the party, none of whom I ever saw again. When I jumped off the truck, to make my way to Royal Naval Barracks, Portsmouth, I assumed that the people who had denounced me for victimizing them would be as glad to see the back of me as I was to be shot of them. When I began to walk away they were greatly shocked and the former trouble-makers were as insistent as any of the others on shaking hands and wishing me luck.

RNB Portsmouth was a very different place from *Collingwood*. The great rambling barracks had been partially gutted – by incendiary bombs if I remember correctly – and it was not looking at its best, whatever that had been like. For the first time in my naval life I slept in a hammock. This allowed the authorities to pack in a lot of people inexpensively. Hammocks proved to be surprisingly convenient and comfortable and since we had been taught how to secure them to their stanchions, no one ended up on the floor. The barracks was essentially a place where people were dumped until they could be sent somewhere else. It would not have been like the navy to leave them to their own devices, in case they got up to mischief, so they were supposed to attend instruction, although no one seemed to take this very seriously and the continual comings and goings made it impossible to plan any meaningful kind of curriculum. On one day I found myself doing six hours' rifle drill, which was an odd way of preparing me for anything that I was likely to encounter.

Provided that one did not try to escape from the barracks itself, evading what passed for tuition posed no great problems. I tried it one day and soon discovered why it was not more common practice. It was simply too strenuous. One obviously had to keep well clear of such traps as the messdeck and the NAAFI canteen. That meant that there was nothing to do except walk, or rather, march, with the brisk and purposeful air of a man on a mission, whenever one spotted gold braid or a petty officer's uniform. Clandestinity also called for alertness and quick thinking. Someone I knew was having a quiet smoke in an air raid shelter when he heard the feet of approaching Authority. Snatching up a providential broom, he sprang smartly to attention and identified himself as a 'surface shelter sweeper'. It was more restful – except when the needle got stuck in the arms drill groove – to snooze at the back of a classroom.

RNB had its compensations. In the first place, my mess was composed entirely of CW ratings and none of us was supposed to be in charge of the others. As a general principle, as I will try to explain later, I deplored this isolation of the gentle-men from the players, but so long as we were merely hanging around, it made it easier to pass the time in congenial company. One met some interesting people and heard of others; like the rating whose parents had left him as a child to be brought up by Amazonian Indians, visiting him once or twice a year. He was said to be a deadly performer on the blowpipe, which suggested that he might have been more usefully employed as a commando, although I doubt if ordnance supplies stretched as far as poisoned arrows.

Another attraction was Ditcham Park. Every evening a coach left for this country house near Petersfield. I never knew who ran the place but they deserve a word of special thanks for their imagination in providing the nearest possible equivalent to every sailor's dream: an 'up-homers'. On arrival at Ditcham everyone was provided with a pair of slippers, a wonderful symbol of emancipation from the world of boots and concrete where you never walked but always marched. After that you did what you liked. There were, if I remember rightly, books and ping-pong tables. There was certainly a quiet room where one could write letters. There was often a film and nothing was compulsory. Ditcham every other night helped to keep us not merely sane but reasonably happy. It was, however, expensive. In present-day terms, 3/6 (17½p) may not seem an excessive price to pay for transport, dinner, bed and break-fast, but it amounted to almost a day and a half's pay. Perhaps that was why there was always plenty of room.

As part of the attempt to fill in our time, we were taken over a Hunt class de-stroyer that was refitting in the dockyard. This was the first time that I had set foot on a ship since joining the navy, and I can remember peeping through a porthole into a cabin and thinking that if that was typical officer's accommodation, there was something to be said for obtaining a commission. In my innocence I did not realize that I had been looking at the captain's cabin. When I was eventually to find myself in a similar ship, I shared with two other officers an area that, as I recall it, was not much bigger than a sleeping compartment on a train.

Another extra-mural excursion occurred when the navy was asked to provide a contingent for a 'warship week' parade in Dorset. It confined its choice to CW rat-ings, presumably on the ground that they had more to lose and were less likely to abscond or get drunk. I was eliminated from the parade itself, since I was told that I rolled when marching, perhaps because I was too tall to accommodate myself to the standard thirty-inch pace. This seemed to me more of a recommendation than a disqualification. Two of us were put in charge of the food supplies, until the petty officers entrusted with the contingent presumably decided that this would be tempt-ing providence. That relegated us to the rôle of tourists, which was all the more attractive since it was very cold and we were able to spend most of our time in a café along the route of the march, merely emerging to form part of the audience at the salute. This was taken by an admiral, who paid a smart tribute to the repre-sentatives of the armed forces, the Home Guard, the Auxiliary Fire Service, the air raid wardens, the first aid people, the decontamination squad (people were still preparing for the use of poisoned gas) and the air cadets. These were followed by the motorised units, which posed problems for the admiral. A fire engine and an ambulance looked pretty clear cases, but a lorry loaded with potatoes was more ambiguous – did it, or did it not represent the allotment holders who were digging for victory? He gave it the benefit of the doubt, but by the time that he found himself saluting bakers' vans and a dust cart he realized that he was dealing with the traffic jam that had built up behind the procession. Being saluted by an admiral must have convinced the dustmen that this was indeed a people's war.

Since no one knew what to do with us, there was plenty of weekend leave and towards the end of November I took advantage of this to nip back to Oxford where my friends, who had opted for the army, were making the most of their borrowed time. Some of their undergraduate antics made me feel like a visiting spectre from the Great Beyond and I probably served them as a kind of *memento mori*. Since officers and other ranks shared the streets of Oxford in roughly equal numbers, an unwritten saluting truce was observed by both sides, who would otherwise have been semaphoring each other every few seconds.

I returned to RNB about one o'clock on Monday afternoon, to hear my name ringing throughout that vast and dismal establishment. I was required to report for draft at four o'clock. I rushed around completing the necessary formalities and finally dashed up several flights of stairs for a medical examination. A surprised doctor asked me if my heart generally behaved like that, and, not realizing that it was responding to my recent marathon, I told him that, to the best of my knowledge, it did. He merely shrugged his shoulders. According to the local folklore they passed you so long as you were still warm.

I left Portsmouth with two petty officers and – a great stroke of luck – four of the CW ratings who had been in the next hut to mine at *Collingwood*. We had been told that we were all destined for HMS *Carnation*, a corvette on the Gibraltar run, which was stationed in Liverpool. That looked like another stroke of good luck. Home was only a couple of hours away and there might be a prospect of leave. When I arrived on board and saw the decks cluttered with the braziers and miscellaneous impedimenta of the dockyard maties, I did not see how the ship could sail for another week. We actually weighed anchor the next day.

I took advantage of the last chance of a night ashore – this time there were no inverted commas. As we left the ship we were told that we had about one cup to every four members of the mess and that it was up to us. I spent the night in some sort of a hostel, determined to prove myself a loyal and reliable shipmate. Oxford, however, had given me no training in either the theory or practice of cup-stealing and I began to fear the worst. After a breakfast that, despite its adequacy in other respects, offered no relevant opportunities, I was going downstairs on my way into the street when, on a landing, in splendid isolation and with no one in sight, there stood a single cup. I have never been much of a believer in a personal providence, but there are times when the balance of the evidence seems to be against me. I have no idea how the others managed, but there was no shortage of cups on that voyage.

CHAPTER 2

THE VIEW FROM THE LOWER DECK

Each of the many corvettes carried a number, prefixed by the letter K. *Carnation* was K00, which suggested that she was the eldest member of that extensive family. I was told that this was not actually the case since 'our engines were bombed in Birmingham'. When I served in the ship she was part of an escort group that took convoys from Liverpool as far as Gibraltar. After that the merchantmen continued on their various ways and the escort group picked up a homeward-bound convoy and brought it back.

Corvettes were the smallest deep-water seagoing ships, not much bigger than ocean-going tugs. I read somewhere that they were 'said to be very lively in a seaway', which was something of an understatement. They rolled all the time, shipped a great deal of spray and the occasional solid water and, in rough weather, were liable to yaw 45° on either side of their intended course. They were essentially fuel tanks and fighting platforms. As in all small ships, the only way from the bows to the stern was along the deck, which was usually wet and sometimes awash. When the weather got really bad we rigged lifelines to avoid being swept overboard.

Seamen were accommodated in two decks in the forecastle, which contained a few bunks and a table or two for our meals. All of the remaining space was occupied by hammocks. The available space had perhaps been adequate in the beginning, but the Admiralty was continually adding new equipment, which needed more seamen to man it, and the resulting congestion must have broken one or two sanitary regulations. Hammocks were comfortable enough in themselves – much more so than bunks, during a north Atlantic winter – and the fact that ours almost touched each other was no great inconvenience, provided that we all rolled together. The overcrowding did, however, mean that there was a good deal of competition for prime sites. I made the mistake of taking a suspiciously empty one that was far too convenient. When the leading seaman who regarded it as his private territory recovered from his hangover, I had to take the only site that was left. This was situated within inches of the navel pipe that carried the anchor cable down from the deck to the cable locker. If the cable had been made really tight, there was no problem. If not, each time the ship rolled, the ironware clanged against the pipe like a bell. It wasn't exactly a lullaby, but when you spent part of every night on watch you learned to sleep through most things.

If the living accommodation was not exactly luxurious, life had its compensations. We had plenty of food, a much more generous ration of 'nutty' (alias chocolate) than civilians got, and vast quantities of rather unpleasant duty-free tobacco. I seem to remember that Martens cigarettes – universally known as 'Bob Martens', after the dogs' conditioning powders – were issued free. Even when the ship was half under water the mess decks were dry and the presence of so many bodies helped to keep them warm. Oddly enough, I can remember nothing of the fug, which must have been overpowering.

We left Liverpool on our own, to rendezvous with the remainder of the escort group in Lough Foyle, Northern Ireland, and within a couple of hours of our sailing I was on the wheel. *Collingwood* had taught me what to do, what orders to expect and how to reply to them, so that posed no great problems and the leading hand in charge of the watch kept a close eye on me. The wheelhouse was warm and dry; we had the sort of compass that would have made Nelson feel at home and all that was expected of me was to keep the ship's head pointing more or less in the right direction. One of the advantages of being in a small ship was that you did a bit of everything and what you didn't know you soon learned. Ordinary seamen were not called upon to do anything very demanding and for much of the time one acted as a kind of odd-job man.

When we came off watch I made myself as comfortable as I could in the forecastle. 'You won't be doing that much longer' said an encouraging shipmate, pointing to my pipe. This puzzled me for a moment until I realized that we were beginning to bounce around as we bashed into a head sea at our top speed, and that I was supposed to feel seasick. I didn't, either then or later, which was convenient. Bad weather was uncomfortable enough without that. Whenever I felt a trifle queasy I used to eat as much as I could. It seemed to settle the stomach.

We had scarcely dropped anchor in Lough Foyle when an invasion flotilla shot out from the Eire side, to barter silk stockings and tins of fruit for duty-free cigarettes. I must have been quite a sanctimonious prig, for I remember being rather shocked by this – until I saw the wardroom steward hard at it, and decided that it was not for me to aspire to higher moral standards than my officers.

This was it. I had survived my first night at sea and become part of the war effort. It was to take me some time to assimilate the tribal culture of *Carnation*, but since that was to condition my present and future reactions, this is as good a place as any for a little anthropology.

There were no RN officers on board, something whose significance I was not to appreciate until the following year. The captain, and perhaps one or two of his officers, came from the merchant navy. I hardly ever encountered him and he remained a Mysterious Presence, to be identified only by the number of rings on his uniform. Like the Olympian gods, he tended to manifest himself to mortals mainly through oracles. He had always to be propitiated but if one performed the appropriate services he was fundamentally benevolent.

The first lieutenant was the only officer on board who was positively disliked, and indeed hated. That was partly his own fault but it is something that tends to happen to first lieutenants. When the captain says 'No. 1, this ship's like a pig sty', it is the first lieutenant who gets the blame for dragging the 'tooth-sucking' crew away from their tobacco, cards and 'zizzes' in order to clean it up.

First lieutenants are the Home Secretaries in the naval polity. Knowing that they can never hope to achieve popularity, they are tempted not to try, and to regard the crew's dislike as the proof that they are doing their job properly. They are also inclined to be houseproud. Our man combined all this with an arrogant air and an unpleasantly sarcastic tongue. The remaining officers – if I remember rightly there were only two of them – were mere shadowy figures who issued orders from time to time.

The only petty officer with whom I had much contact was the Chief Boatswain's Mate, or 'Buffer', who was a man who had an opinion about most things. Someone told me that he initially took a dislike to me because he knew – goodness knows how – that I had been at Oxford. I won him over by my sedulous attentions: the habit of bawling 'Morning, Buffs!' when I saw him for the first time each day. He made a point of replying, when he could discover where I was, and if this was painting the funnel or perched in the crow's nest halfway up the mast, it could take him quite a long time. These games of hide and seek convinced him that I was not disposed to be socially exclusive and we got on well enough for me to be able to tease him. Towards the end of my time on board he once asked me to pass him the string.

'When I was at *Collingwood*, Buffs, they taught us there was no such thing as string in the navy. It's called codline.'

'When you've been in the navy as long as I have, if you want there to be string there is string.'

The seamen were divided into red, white and blue watches. I forget the colour of mine, but it was presided over by Leading Seaman Len Bowen, with whom I got on very well. I don't know why Len had joined the navy, in the years before the war, and he probably wished that he hadn't. None of the things one associates with sailors seemed to have anything to do with him, although he was perfectly proficient at his job. He gave the impression of being a quiet, regular, home-loving kind of family man with a melancholy disposition that circumstances had done nothing to counterbalance. He had had a daughter who was born after he had sailed for the China station. When he returned to England at the end of the commission she was already dead. Len was easy-going, but possessed of formidable linguistic resources that one would not have suspected. His rôle on watch was a supervisory one – in other words, he sat in the warmth of the wheelhouse and chatted with whoever was doing a stint on the wheel. Halfway through a night watch he would go down below and brew up kye (cocoa to the uninitiated) for his little team of four or five men. One night he discovered that the previous watch had forgotten to wash up their cups. Len came straight back to the wheelhouse and, without any explanation, proceeded to curse Churchill for what seemed a very long time, without pausing for breath and without ever repeating himself. I had the good luck to be on the wheel at the time and I was spellbound. I have never heard anything like it since.

Having a long-standing preference for a quiet life over an adventurous one, I was glad to be in Len's watch rather than in that of the mercurial Sid (if he had a surname, I never heard anyone mention it). Sid was a wizened and gnome-like character. He was a man of many talents and I have heard him play tunes through the metal piece at the end of a hosepipe. His more Homeric achievements had taken place before I joined the ship. People were still talking about the memorable occasion when *Carnation* was in dry-dock, propped up by more or less loose beams, and Liverpool was being heavily bombed; a combination of circumstances that might have been expected to concentrate the minds of those involved on questions of mortality. One night Sid assembled a little party on the quayside and marched them off, with the maximum of clatter, to a nearby warehouse, where he stood them noisily at ease. A reluctant head emerged from the hut at the far end of the yard and wanted to know what was going on.

'Didn't they tell you? They're expecting a heavy raid tonight – you saw that convoy that came in this afternoon. So they're doubling up on the fire-watching. You seem to have a cosy little place there.'

'That's right. It's nice and warm. Since it's all quiet me and the mates were just having a game of cards but I suppose we'd better come out and join you.'

'No use all of us playing at silly buggers and we've got no choice. You get back to your cards and we'll let you know right away if it looks as though the balloon's going up.'

'That's very decent of you. Let us know when you want a cup of tea.'

When the official fire-watchers eventually realized that their accommodating auxiliaries had vanished, they raised the alarm. *Carnation* was searched from end to end and from top to bottom but they never got even a sniff of the whisky from that warehouse.

I was present one day when the captain fell in the crew and announced that one or two of them had received commendations for their exploits on the voyage just before I joined the ship. I seem to remember that Sid had been mentioned in despatches. When the convoy had been attacked by a submarine, HMS *Cossack* had been torpedoed and badly damaged. The rest of the convoy sailed on, leaving *Carnation* to stand by the abandoned destroyer until a tug could be sent to tow her into Gibraltar. The captain called for volunteers to board *Cossack*, which was liable to sink at any time and Sid was the first to come forward. He made his way straight down to the wardroom where he found that the spirit cupboard was unlocked, and they almost had to drag him back to his own ship. This set the pattern for the next day or two. Sid was always the first to respond to the call and the last to return to safety. When *Cossack* sank before they could get her into Gibraltar, the general feeling on board *Carnation* was that the loss of that famous ship was to be deeply regretted, but that it saved the posing of some awkward questions. I think Sid's commendation was for conspicuous devotion to duty.

Geographically speaking, the crew ranged from a Stornoway fisherman so softly spoken as to be virtually inaudible, to Alfie the cockney. It included some rough customers but we were not a bunch of illiterates – I recall some of my messmates being scandalized by the goings-on in one of Graham Greene's novels. When I looked round the mess one night at sea I noticed that the St. Andrews graduate was reading a French novel, my friend Dennis Moore was deep into something in German and I was making what I could out of a medieval Latin chronicle about my current hero, Simon de Montfort. I remember a couple of coders, the elder of whom seemed to regard himself as the custodian of the Delphic oracle. He was inclined to treat every signal as though it were a private communication from the Admiralty. He was said to have worked in a bank, which perhaps helped to explain his concern for confidentiality. His more communicative partner, who had been a conductor on a Midland Red bus, was said to nurse the improbable ambition of becoming a gentleman's gentleman after the war. By this time the Admiralty was very well informed about the position of the numerous German U-boat packs. As retailed by the coders, our part of the Atlantic seemed to be so full of them that we were in danger of collision. Many years later, when I saw the German film, *Das Boot* it came as something of

Alfie, the Cockney crew member of Carnation.

a shock when I realized that the submarine involved had been looking for me! I was hailed as a townee by a stoker from Bolton who took me to look at his boiler but I didn't see much of him since stokers had their own mess with a tribal life and a mentality of their own. They seemed to be inclined to melancholy and they had their own folksongs which combined a peculiarly earthy obscenity with a sense of cosmic doom.

There was also Peter Warwick, who was in my own watch. Since Peter took a rather large size in hats he was universally known as 'bomb head'. He was a somewhat tense individual who was liable to bursts of passionate invective on unexpected subjects, such as the profligacy of the 1942 New Year Honours List which he told me included virtually the entire population except 'you and me and my oppo'. He also had a sense of the dramatic. He once told me that if we were 'fished' (torpedoed), what I should need was not a life jacket but a parachute.

Peter was almost paranoid on a subject that sent cold shivers down everyone's spines: the hatred and dread of all things 'pusser'. Since pusserdom will form a kind of *leitmotif* to a good deal of this narrative, I must try to convey as powerfully as I can, not merely its lexicographical meaning but the intensity of the feelings that it aroused. This will not be easy since there was no exact equivalent in the comparatively impoverished patois of the other two services. It is not to be confused with 'bull', which has passed into general usage. Bull implies a kind of bluff, a cheerful attempt to pass off illusions as realities. Pusser was altogether more comprehensive and more sinister.

The word is, of course, a corruption of 'purser', which implies big ship bureaucracy. The idea of a purser in a ship like *Carnation* would have been as surreal as that of a boy bugler. When, much later, I was responsible for a liaison crew of half a dozen men, I had to submit a monthly complement return, and was presented with vast forms that seemed to have been intended for first world war battleships. They began with boy buglers and I had to resist the temptation to include one or two and see if anyone noticed. This, however, is to digress. By extension, pusser had come to signify the kind of mores and attitudes that one associated with the kind of ships that carried pursers. Spit and polish became ends in themselves and doing things in the textbook way took precedence over getting the right results. It was an invasive mentality that drove the pusser to try to regulate every aspect of other people's lives in accordance with King's Regulations and Admiralty Instructions. I can perhaps best illustrate what I mean by a couple of examples.

Corvettes had solid bulwarks with hinged scuppers that allowed the water to escape overboard when the decks were awash. Our pusser first lieutenant decided that these detracted from the smooth lines of the bulwarks, and had them welded shut. On my second voyage we found ourselves in a tremendous following gale and the masses of water that we shipped were trapped on the upper deck. The seaman's mess, with its habitual penchant for the ghoulish, made its blood curdle with the tale of a tug that was alleged to have capsized for just this reason. By this time we had a new first lieutenant who ordered the scuppers to be bashed open with a sledgehammer and we lived to tell the tale.

A year or so after I left *Carnation*, an RN lieutenant who had been the only member of his mess to survive when the Japanese sank the *Prince of Wales* and the *Repulse*, told me that he was dreading the end of the war.

'You've no idea how the navy's run in peacetime. An ordinary seaman is painting something or other, watched by a leading seaman, who is being watched by a petty officer, who is being watched by a sub-lieutenant, who is being watched by the officer of the day. They are all scared stiff because, if the seaman spills one drop of paint on the deck, that will mean a black mark in the record of each of them.'

It passed for dogma in *Carnation* that the paradise of pusserdom was the naval gunnery school at Whale Island, near Portsmouth, where all evolutions were performed at the double and everyone ran instead of marching. From their point of view it was a kind of hell to which fate might condemn them at any time. We had a crow's nest, a kind of metal barrel halfway up the mast. When there was a heavy sea running – which was most of the time in the north Atlantic in winter – the man in the crow's nest acquired a new insight into the experience of being 'rocked in the cradle of the deep'. Into the paintwork of this crow's nest an anonymous hand had carved a terrible curse: 'Whale Island for bomb-head Warwick'.

Pusserdom seemed to have an irresistible appeal to a certain kind of RN officer – I am writing of the 1940s and things are no doubt very different today. My messmates were inclined to assume that big ships, especially those they always described as 'battle-wagons', were inevitably pusser. They had the time, they were certainly not short of labour and they were officered by people to whom pusserdom came naturally. Small ships, continually at sea and run by men from the merchant navy or recent civilians, had neither the time nor the inclination to be pusser. *Carnation* was a typical example. In pusser ships hammocks were stowed away every morning but ours remained slung all the time we were at sea. We wore whatever clothing we found convenient, usually boiler suits, and our only concession to the solemnity of 'harbour stations' was to put on our naval caps. Our merchant navy officers took all this in their stride. Some small ships invested sartorial informality with an imaginative touch that bordered on the sublime. During the landing in Sicily I saw an armed trawler where every man on deck was wearing a trilby. It said a lot about their morale.

Life at sea in a corvette was inevitably uncomfortable. An eminent criminologist whom I met when I was on leave in Oxford, once said to me that, unless they were to fall back on racks and thumbscrews, the authorities had to rely on our patriotism to discourage us from deserting. 'You'd be rather more comfortable in gaol and very much safer.' On the whole the crews accepted this danger and discomfort with no more than routine grumbling. What made them almost homicidal was being made to sacrifice their scanty leisure for fatuous reasons of officiousness or display. The only time that I was ever made to holystone a deck was immediately before our major refit, when *Carnation* was about to be handed over to dockyard maties who were rarely punctilious about wiping their boots, and that part of the deck was about to disappear anyway. I suppose it was meant to keep me out of mischief.

When you had experienced all this from below you were inoculated against pusserdom, unless you were a rather peculiar kind of person. When you became an officer, unlike the gentlemen from Dartmouth, you knew just what the lads on the lower deck were thinking. This posed a potential threat to the traditions of the service. I heard that, towards the end of the war, Their Lordships at the Admiralty woke up to the danger of exposing future officers to the attitudes of the lower deck and segregated them in training cruisers. There could have been other reasons for that, but we took it for granted that the intention was to prevent them from absorbing the 'bolshie' attitudes of the lower deck. This had its drawbacks since it also meant that they could not understand seamen's language. In 1945 I met a newly-commissioned liaison officer who was experiencing this difficulty. When someone reported to him that the W/T set had 'fallen over' (i.e. broken down) he offered to send help to pick it up. Since he didn't know enough French to understand what the French officers were saying either, he was a little isolated.

If I am right about the intentions of the Admiralty, they knew what they were doing. Once you had absorbed anti-pusserdom it was with you for life. Looking back on forty years as a university teacher, it sometimes seems to me that, for better or worse, it has been my constant guide. A pusser-detector, which I conceive as a kind of metaphysical Geiger counter, is a very useful instrument for identifying those who lose track of the ends in their obsessional preoccupation with the propriety of the means.

It is not easy to explain what crews do in wartime, on board ships that are usually at sea and very rarely in contact with the enemy. Where *Carnation* was concerned, most of our time on watch was spent acting as look-outs. This involved scouring the sea and sky for ships, submarines and aircraft and, so far as I was concerned, never seeing any of them. By day, this tended to be somewhat lacking in variety; by night, when one could scarcely make out the convoy and the other escorts, it was even less exciting. W.S. Gilbert knew what he was talking about when he wrote

> When all night long a chap remains
> On sentry go, to chase monotony,
> He exercises all his brains –
> That is, assuming that he's got any.

The worst look-out position was by the pom-pom, since it faced aft and you couldn't even see where you were going, but only where you had been. It did, however, have the virtue of privacy, which had a certain scarcity value. My first solution to the problem of finding something to do with my fifty-minute sessions by the pom-pom was to whistle my own symphony concerts, but since I wasn't very good on the developmental passages, I soon exhausted my repertoire. After that I took to composing love sonnets to an imaginary Amaryllis. A fifty-minute spell was just about right for one of those, but after two or three of them I ran out of inspiration. After that I just looked where the sea was supposed to be.

During the forenoons we did odd jobs, making the less unpleasant ones last as long as possible. In harbour we painted. The army used to say, 'If it moves, salute it; if it doesn't move, paint it,' but I got the impression that we painted it whether it moved or not. One day three or four of us were detailed off to paint the ship's side.

When we announced to the petty officer in charge that we couldn't do this since there was another corvette alongside, he looked at us with contempt and told us to push it out of the way, so we did. After all, it only weighed about 900 tons. I wished that Archimedes could have seen us. We then stood on a plank that had been lowered a bit too far, so that it was just under water, and a shoal of tiny fish played around our sea boots. One of our RNVR officers who was leaning over the side, suggested that they were testing us for flavour, which struck us as being in rather doubtful taste.

Life on the messdeck was certainly a liberal education. To begin with, one had to learn the language. This was not just a matter of talking about decks and deck-heads rather than floors and ceilings. All kinds of things, whether they were associated with the navy or not, had different names. Cigarettes were 'ticklers' since the duty-free issue was supplied in tins that had once reminded somebody of Tickler's jam. A soldier on board a ship was a 'pongo'. All duty-

In the navy we painted it, whether it moved or not.

free goods of any description were known as rabbits. If one saw a sailor going ashore with his ditty box, one called after him, 'Tuck its ears in.' We had our own picturesque turns of phrase: a man who had found himself out of his depth would say 'There was I, like a whore at a christening.' Anything protracted went on 'from arse holes to breakfast time'. Like other folk languages, that of the navy had a kind of instinctive rightness that defied rational analysis. When a playful wave came over the side and jumped down your neck, the only comment that brought any relief was a long drawn out 'Baaaaastard!' I have tried others and can testify to their inferiority.

Learning the vocabulary was, of course, only the beginning. One had to acquire the idiom and the folklore. The latter was usually either pessimistic or self-deprecatory or both.

> This is my story, this is my song,
> We've been in commission too bloody long.
> Then roll on the *Nelson*, the *Rodney* and *Hood*,
> This one-funnelled bastard is no bloody good.

When the *Hood* was sunk by the *Bismarck* the last couplet was promptly altered to

> Then roll on the *Nelson*, the *Rodney*, *Renown*,
> You can't have the *Hood* 'cos the bugger's gone down.

'Roll on my twelve!' was a frequent invocation, referring to the period for which people had signed up. Our lower deck had almost a passion for the mock-heroic:

> Bang went the four-inch for'ard,
> Crash went the pom-pom aft;
> Down came the bloody funnel,
> Away went the after mast.

One of our many incantations was 'Gunnels under? She was fucking funnels under!' Almost any reference to one's previous activities would produce cries of 'Stand up, Jack' or 'What ship, Jack?'

This bardic culture knew all about heroic epithets, repetition and the recital of texts whose every world was enshrined by tradition. I wish I could recall more of them. All I can remember of one of these epics is 'The bosun, crafty bastard that he was ...' which, I am afraid, leaves the plot somewhat obscure. We already knew about the 'waga-waga bird which, when pursued, flies round and round in ever-diminishing circles and finally disappears up its own stern orifice, whence it hoots and toots derisively at its pursuers'. I heard songs in *Carnation* that I never heard anywhere else.

> Now some say old Hitler took Warsaw
> And some say he's taken Tilsit,
> But all that he'll ever got from Poland
> Is handfuls and handfuls of ...
> Sweet violets,
> Sweeter than all the roses,
> Covered all over from head to toe,
> Covered all over in snow.
>
> Now some say old Hitler's an airman
> And some say he knows quite a bit,
> But one day he made a forced landing
> And fell in a field full of ...
> Sweet violets ...
>
> Now some say old Hitler is dead now
> And some say he died in a fit
> And some say they'll bury him in ashes

But I say they'll bury him in …
Sweet violets …

And now that my story is ended,
About Hitler you know quite a bit
And if the old bastard should come down your way
You can pelt him with handfuls of …
Sweet violets …

There was a fair amount of talk about homosexuality, but no action. Friends were inclined to address each other as 'bash' and 'wings' and anyone was liable to chant

'If you'll be my winger I'll be your old man,
I'll do all your dhobeying …'

'Dhobeying', which had presumably been picked up on the India station, meant washing clothes, as in

'Dhobey, dhobey, dhobey, never go ashore,
Never have to muster at the Sick Bay door.'

Another favourite recital went: 'And when Nabob the son of Paybob was going from Pompey (Portsmouth) to Southsea with the petty cash, he fell amongst thieves, who ragged him and bagged him and shagged him, and sent him on his way rejoicing.' It was all a pose. A previous CW rating was said to have invited his friends into his bunk and they were still discussing whether or not he could possibly have meant it.

Somewhat in contrast, I witnessed a moving naval tradition. A member of the ship's company had died before I came on board and when we were in Gibraltar his few remaining effects were put up for auction. His former shipmates were not content just to bid them up to excessive prices, in order to help his widow. As often as not, they put them back into the auction to be sold again. This sometimes happened two or three times.

I do not want to romanticize. We were always uncomfortable and for much of the time we were cold and wet. We never got enough sleep and the idea of privacy was a bad joke. These were not conditions that made for good humour, mutual tolerance or social harmony. We were not jolly sailorboys, united by the brotherhood of the sea. I remember a particularly evil occasion when some of his messmates taunted Len Bowen in the hope that he could be goaded into hitting one of them, which would have allowed them to get him stripped of his leading seaman's rank, pay and pension. Len was perfectly aware of what they were trying to do and he refused to play their game, but this manifestation of raw hatred was something not easily forgotten. It was more or less a matter of luck whether the crew directed their outbreaks of temper against the sea, the navy or each other. No one ever referred to the Germans. I got the impression that the general feeling was that they were up against it in the same way as us. Seamen were often selfish but they could be generous in big or little things. One or two of my messmates offered me 'sippers' of their rum ration when they knew that I could not repay them since I was 'under age' and not entitled to any grog. On the whole we were held together by our shared fate and I learned that one could put up with a good amount of material discomfort and casual bad temper. I could identify with their feelings and we had more in common than appeared at first sight. It is only when one finds one's self amongst people with wholly incompatible principles that things break down.

The tale of our adventures is soon told. We left Liverpool on 26 November 1941 and arrived at Gibraltar about a fortnight later. Convoys in those days were very slow and we had to sail far into the Atlantic to escape the reconnaissance aircraft that would have guided the submarines in our direction. Family friends, who had been on pre-war cruises that took a couple of days to get to what they called 'Gib' could not imagine what we had been doing all that time. My own longest voyage had been from Fleetwood to the Isle of Man; so, by the time we reached our destination I was beginning to feel that I had been born on board.

Day after day all that we did was stare at the convoy and at the surrounding sea and sky. In bad weather everything looked fairly chaotic and it was only when the sea calmed down that one became aware of the pattern made by the merchant ships and their escorts. Nothing happened to us, but there had been plenty of action on previous trips, and the other escort group that shared the Liverpool to Gibraltar run with us seemed to be fighting submarines all the time. On convoy duty you never know when you are in the presence of the enemy and almost anything can happen at any time. I tried to sum it all up in a poem about what I might have experienced.

Convoy

The wind is quiet now, low pregnant clouds
Darken the plains of the sea, but no one sleeps.
The plaintive sirens of the dim-seen convoy
Open the gates of pity like the cry
Of frightened animals when horror glares
Green-eyed, from the black forest all around.

To each of us, closed up at action stations,
The wailing sirens call a special tune –
Sheep on the rocky slopes of clouded fells

In Cumberland, cows in the sun-drenched fields
Of Oxfordshire on summer afternoons,
Loved earth re-planted in sea-wearied hearts –
Then a torpedo shatters the still night.
For some of us there is no homecoming.

There is no righteous anger; only hatred.
Pity those sweating in their fumy cells,
Exiles from stars and winds of evening,
Dreaming, like us, of home; all warped and gnarled
By their world's rottenness – to call them guilty
Is jangling broken words to no sane end.

Think, till morality gives way to tears,
Of women weeping the long lonely night
In sleepy German towns the tourist loved,
Prisoners pacing each her cell of fear
Within the skull, her daily agony
The postman's knock each morning.

Only by pity, the obstinate heart
That dares be human, may we hope to clean
Some blood from our red fingers, murderers all,
All whom their hearts' consent binds to the war
Share in the killing: spinster patriots,
The parson urging heaven to mobilize,
The pacifist, with all his reservations,
Harvesting fields that blood has fertilized.

And now the sea peels silently astern
Into the tattered dawn, and now to leave
Enigmas labyrinthine unresolved.
Time's children, all our seeking only yields
Contemporary truth – eyes in the dark;
Chasing the ultimate Grail of good and ill
All vanity and labour lost. We keep
The truest course by the best light we know.

Not Really What You'd Call a War

There was not a great deal to do in Gibraltar but at least we stopped rolling and we could sleep all night. Just up the road Franco was still denouncing democracy and there was a feeling of being under siege. I was rather surprised by the extent to which he was loathed by everyone who had served in the navy before the war, until I realized that this was the product of chauvinism rather than of ideology. What incensed them was the fact that, during the Spanish civil war, when Franco's warships fired on British merchantmen, all that the British warships on 'non-intervention patrol' were allowed to do was to sail between them, when they were itching to blow the Spanish ships out of the water for their impertinence. There were some Spaniards working in the dockyard, whom one of our crew used to greet with 'Franco … bastardo!' I suppose he thought that it was the best he could do.

There was not much to buy in the shops, apart from things that I could not afford, like the 'real genuine Satsuma ware, seven times burnt into fire'. It was a surprise to discover that most of the shopkeepers seemed to be Indian. A messmate explained to me that it took time for the odd merchant ship that had put into Gibraltar with us to get its cargo into the shops, so that we could buy it up and take it back to England. Even at the time, that struck me as a rather oversimplified explanation of the operation of the wartime economy.

After a few days we went out on a local patrol. When I was on watch that night I was suddenly overwhelmed by the conviction that I was about to die - I could not be sure why, but I felt quite certain about the fact. I got Len's permission to go down to the 'heads'. It was perhaps an odd place to choose for my departure from this world but it turned out to be an appropriate one. We got very short of vitamin C during the war and just before we sailed I had been taking rather excessive advantage of the abundance of local fruit …

Christmas Day was rather good fun. All the messdecks were decorated with signal flags and balloons and we were treated to pork and plum pudding. During the evening two of our officers put on ratings' uniforms and we formed a band and carol party which boarded one or two neighbouring ships in pursuit of free drink. Some were co-operative but there was some kind of a civic reception taking place on board the pusser landing ship, *Ulster Monarch*, and they threw us out. Our first lieutenant, of all people, rallied his troops and organized a counterattack, for which much may be forgiven him. Eventually they paid us Danegeld in food and drink on condition that we went away.

We were back in Liverpool by mid-January, after another uneventful convoy. My watch was not the lucky one that got two or three days' leave, but everyone rallied round to make sure that I got a sight of home. I was allowed to act as quartermaster; and the quartermasters then went into twenty-four hour shifts, to give me a whole day off. Home leave was sacred and if you couldn't get it yourself you did what you could to help other people.

What I remember best about that brief stay in Liverpool is that getting back to the ship after a night ashore seemed rather more dangerous than escorting convoys. *Carnation* was lying in Gladstone Dock. This was a rambling and unpopular berth since the Customs and Excise men who manned the gates were said to have a keen eye for 'rabbits'. The policemen who kept watch over the smaller docks were liable to find urgent business somewhere else when they saw seamen approaching the gates. The complex of quays and stretches of oily water that comprised Gladstone Dock posed more serious problems. To find the entrance you made what you hoped was an appropriate selection amongst the gates in an interminable brick wall. You then had to find your way – in the blackout of course – through all the anchor cables and miscellaneous junk that littered the quays. It probably helped if you were sober, although it made you more aware of the penalty for failing to complete the course. With their usual penchant for the macabre, my messmates regaled themselves with tales of bodies found floating in the oily water, but we didn't suffer any casualties.

On January 25 we were off again, in icy weather. My job, as we went down the Mersey was to stow the forward mooring rope, which was hard as iron, in neat coils under the 4" gun platform. That was difficult enough but worse was to follow. We dropped our anchor in Lough Foyle after another stormy passage. There was no problem about that. The difficulties began when we raised it. Gentle reader, if you have ever watched a ship weighing anchor, it has probably never occurred to you to wonder what happens to that length of cable when it comes on board. I am in a position to tell you, at least where flower class corvettes are concerned. It passes through the navel pipe down to the cable locker where a rating with an iron hook stows it away in tidy loops … at least in theory. On that wretched occasion the unfortunate rating was me. What happened was not entirely my fault. As we had battered our way to Lough Foyle against the usual head sea we had flooded the cable locker and fused the light, so that I was operating in total darkness. I could not keep up with the remorseless flow of cable and once things got out of control they went from bad to worse. There was nothing for it but to pay out the cable and start again. This is not the kind of thing that captains like. It makes them feel conspicuous. It says a great deal for ours that, although he did not forget it, he did not summon me to the bridge to tell me about his feelings.

The weather was even worse than on our previous voyage. After three days the senior officer of the escort signalled 'Convoy doing 2½ knots. Keep pinging (sending out asdic emissions to detect submarines) and pray for better weather'. On February 5 the escort was reinforced by two destroyers, in the middle of the night. These escaped detection by our radar, which was perhaps not surprising, since we had a fixed radar aerial which spanned a narrow arc in front of the ship; if you wanted to look in any other direction you had to turn the whole ship! The destroyers also escaped detection by the signalman on the bridge and by the forward lookout – no prizes are offered for guessing who *he* was! They were eventually picked up by the asdic operator, who was supposed to be looking for submarines. It was just as well that they were friendly.

On one of our short excursions from Gibraltar the captain decided that it was time to test his depth charges. It was easy enough to kill or stun the fish; the problem was to get them on board before the gannets grabbed them. Everything was pressed into service, including a wastepaper basket tied to the end of a pole. This broke loose and I liked to think of it being retrieved in Spain by a German agent who would report that British shipping losses were on the increase.

On another occasion we hit a freak wave during the night. *Carnation* heeled over and hung there for a few seconds. The bump woke me up and I turned to ask the leading seaman in the next hammock what was going on … only to find that he was already out on deck. He had been in enough tight spots to know what it might have been. It is easy to be cheerful and unconcerned when you are fresh and ignorant. Experience is wearing and even if you are lucky, years of escape and attrition sap your resistance.

On the voyage home we ran with a great following gale. My messmates welcomed that, arguing that it might add a couple of knots to the speed of the convoy although, as one of them explained to me, the return trip always took longer since we were going uphill. In weather like that the ship was virtually impossible to steer, yawing through as much as 80° to either side of our course and from time to time we had to go round in a circle, to regain our proper position in the escort screen. This time we came up the Irish Sea and since this was regarded as more dangerous than passing to the west of Ireland, we posted a lookout on the forecastle. One night of that has left me with a permanent scepticism about the efficiency of long johns.

Just off Liverpool the convoy broke up, most of the ships entering the port. We, however, were detailed off to escort one of them to Barrow. It was getting late and Liverpool would soon be closed for the night. The captain waited until the senior officer of the escort was out of the way and then approached our merchantman.

'You know the way to Barrow don't you? And you won't be wanting an escort … Full speed ahead.'

That meant that we could all look forward to a night in our bunks. Not an early one though; our protesting coder, who doubled up as postman, was packed off to grope his way through the blackout to the Fleet Mail Office. Next to leave, there was nothing so sacred as mail.

We knew that we were due for a major refit. That did not mean that we would get one. In the navy, nothing could be relied on until it happened and there was an alarming rumour that *Bluebell's* boiler had moved. That might allow her to jump the queue. On the optimistic assumption that everything would work out for the best, we ran a book on where the happy event would take place. I was rather relieved to lose since I had drawn Milford Haven. In the end all went well and we were ordered to North Shields. We left Liverpool on March 8 to circumnavigate the north of Scotland. Nowadays people pay quite a lot of money to do that kind of thing. They do it in more comfort but they are very lucky indeed if they get weather like ours. The sun shone all day and the whole of Scotland was under deep snow. I had scarcely distinguished myself on our last trip, with my dismal performance in the cable locker and my failure to spot the destroyers. This time I was a superb look-out. Sweeping the Cuillins with my powerful 1900A binoculars, I picked up aircraft many miles away, even if no one seemed very interested. The north coast of Scotland looked like my idea of Greenland; it seemed virtually uninhabited. I tried to kindle some enthusiasm in the 'Buffer' for the superb prospect, but he said that he would sooner be sitting in a pub in Birmingham. As usual, we worked ourselves up into a state of some apprehension about the raging seas to be expected in the Pentland Firth, only to find that there was scarcely a ripple on the water.

Once in North Shields we slaved away without the usual 'tooth-sucking', unloading all our ammunition, and on the 14th I said goodbye to the ship on 25 days' leave – half a lifetime by wartime standards. I had not quite completed my statutory three months' 'sea time' but the captain was not the man to fuss about details. He summoned his five CW ratings and expressed his general satisfaction with our performance even if from my own point of view, he rather spoiled the effect by saying that he did not propose to make an issue of the cable locker business. One of my happiest recollections of the war is sitting in the incredible luxury of sole occupancy of a third-class railway compartment and watching Durham cathedral slide by the window. I knew that I should miss my last train from Manchester and could look forward to a night in a waiting room, but that was nothing to set against almost a month at home, the prospect of a summer ashore and a commission at the end of it. Since then I have passed Durham cathedral more times than I care to remember, and never without recalling that magical evening.

That was not quite the end of my association with *Carnation*. Nine months later, the commanding officer of the destroyer in which I was serving received a letter from someone in the Directory of Navy Accounts at Bath with a sense of humour that one did not expect from a paybob. 'You appear to have an officer on board who is in the habit of not paying his mess bills…' The bill in question had been drawn up after I left *Carnation* and it presented the navy accounts people with quite a problem. It was first directed to Portsmouth, where they had lost track of me since I was no longer an ordinary seaman. Plymouth and Chatham quite understandably said that they knew nothing about me. Some genius wrote on the envelope 'Try Royal Naval Patrol Service Rosyth' but that drew a blank too. The demand for payment eventually ended up in Bath, where they knew everything. The sum involved was 1/3d or just over 5p. Of course, money was worth more in those days and postage was cheap, but it must have cost quite a few man-hours to recover that 5p. I may have been inclined to make the odd criticism about the navy's way of doing things but I can't deny that it was thorough.

CHAPTER 3

CHANGING WORLDS

I have very little recollection of how I spent the spring and summer of 1942. As I graduated from ordinary seaman to officer cadet and eventually to sub-lieutenant, and waited to be admitted to various training courses, I spent about half of my time on home leave. That meant no diary and no letters to my parents. I must have felt that I was living on borrowed time and tried to make the most of every minute but I have no idea what that implied. The weeks that the navy claimed were quite unlike anything else in my wartime experience. To begin with, we lived in a kind of limbo; we were not yet officers but when petty officers wanted us to do something they said 'Please'. Apart from the inevitable 'field training' it was like being back at school. We spent our days sitting at desks and absorbing theoretical information about things like pilotage and navigation, mines and torpedoes. There was plenty of weekend and evening leave, which allowed me to slip up to London and to explore the Sussex countryside. I was not to know that this was to be my last summer in England until the end of the war, but I must have felt that my luck was too good to last.

I returned to Portsmouth barracks on my twentieth birthday, early in April, and settled back into the familiar routine. For some mysterious reason the authorities seemed to be living in hourly expectation of a German landing, or perhaps they invented an invasion scare in order to find something for us to do. We turned out at all hours of the day and night, in response to 'double red' alerts and spent much of our time preparing to defend such parts of the barracks as had not already been destroyed, on the optimistic assumption that the enemy would have been provided with nothing more lethal than rifles.

My hammock had gone missing between North Shields and Portsmouth, so I was given a chit authorizing me to draw a replacement from the stores. This took me into a strange region of the barracks, past dustbins labelled 'Ullage', 'Dry Sullage' and 'Wet Sullage', terms as mysterious to me now as they were then, which I was never to see again during the war. When I eventually found the hammock store two ratings materialized, apparently from hibernation, looked at my chit and threw on the floor a depressing assortment of dirty and tattered bits of canvas, pieces of string and unidentifiable objects. I was contemplating this with some dismay when one of them said, 'Of course, if you were to let us have half a crown and come back later this afternoon, we'd make you up a hammock ourselves, from the newest and cleanest stuff we've got.' It was a day's pay well spent since it saved me a laborious scrubbing job for which my old hammock was long overdue.

A week after my return to barracks, I was summoned before a preliminary board for what was more of a chat than a serious interview. They began by asking me if *Carnation* smelt as sweetly as her name. That was not very difficult to answer. They even took a sympathetic interest in my poetical aspirations – war poetry was quite a respectable occupation – but when they asked me what I hoped to do after the war I thought it safer to switch to journalism. They seemed to like that too and in the end they passed me. In view of the kind of questions that they had asked, it would have been difficult for them to do anything else.

The monotonous routine was broken by a memorable trip to London, where I appeared with Lieutenant Laurence Olivier, as he then was, at the Albert Hall. Modesty compels me to admit that I shared this distinction with several hundred other people and that his rôle was rather more conspicuous than mine. The *Daily Express*, which was campaigning for an early landing in occupied Europe, had organized a patriotic pageant for St. George's Day, to which all the services were invited to contribute. True to form, the navy chose its contingent entirely from CW ratings. Our little band was certainly well-behaved but it was perhaps a little lacking in belligerency. During a rehearsal the director called the various service contingents to join him on the floor of the hall. The RAF people leapt to their feet and doubled into the arena. The men from the army did not bother to use the aisles but scrambled over the seats like gorillas. 'Thank you. And now the navy.' Nothing happened for a moment or two and then a rather languid youth got to his feet and drawled, 'I say, has anyone seen a gash rifle?' The men from the forces were not due to do their marching until after the end of the pageant proper. Most of us would then just parade up and down, followed by an élite formation – of which I was not a member – which was to simulate an assault. On the night of the show we were dumped out of the way, behind a huge banner of St. George and his dragon, which meant that we could see nothing at all except the back of the banner. That was a mistake on the part of the management. The élite formation, who were sitting on the front rows, promptly fixed bayonets and a series of narrow slits appeared in the banner. That solved their problem but it was of no use to the rest of us so we began to stamp. When agitated officials failed to stop us they had to find us places where we could see the rest of the show. I was not greatly impressed by the selective view of 'Our Island Story' and revolted by the crude and hysterical attempt to conscript the Almighty on the allied side. The audience reserved its most enthusiastic applause for the non-combatants, the merchant navy and the nurses, which seemed to the rest of us to be a very healthy reaction.

By the end of April I was back home on indefinite leave, calling at Oxford on the way, where I took a couple of wickets for my old college, against the Radcliffe Infirmary. Civilian life seemed only just round the corner. Towards the end of May the navy remembered me and recalled me to duty. I had now finished with Portsmouth barracks and I was lodged in a boarding house at Hove, which was a distinct improvement in all kinds of ways. After a couple of days I went before another board. This was a much more serious affair and I misunderstood a question about the brakes on a capstan, which I could have answered if I had known what they were getting at. When they asked me if *Carnation* had experienced any difficulties, as a single-screw ship, Len Bowen came to my rescue. With just such a situation in mind, he had told me about our 'kick to port when going astern'. Not being quite sure what that meant, I could not hope to express it more technically, but they seemed to be satisfied with this rather informal definition of transverse thrust. Thirty of us went before the board and twenty-eight passed, so they were not being unduly rigorous.

This was the real dividing line. Henceforth we were genuine cadets and the presumption was that almost all of us would soon be officers and, of course, gentlemen. We were still not supposed to mix socially with those who already sported gold rings on their sleeves, but we had emerged from the lower deck. We were no longer assumed to be naturally criminous and in need of supervision and restraint. It was rather like the transition from school to university, or at least into the sixth form.

Early in June we were transferred to Lancing College for five weeks. We were worked hard, since we had a lot to learn about a wide variety of subjects. Ships are complicated contraptions and officers of the watch are supposed to be able to cope with everything except the engines. Our periods of instruction fell into two different categories. The more abstract subjects, like pilotage and navigation, were taught by officers who lectured to us as though we were undergraduates. The more technical side of things – gunnery, signalling, mines and torpedoes was left to petty officers, who tended to do things by rote. They had their own way of being pusser. What mattered was not giving a correct explanation of something, but doing it by the approved formula. Our gunnery instructor began by asking us 'What is a gun?' He allowed the increasingly imaginative answers to accumulate for some time before he went on 'You're all wrong. A gun is a chube.' On the day before our final examination the torpedo instructor gave us some helpful advice. 'When you come to do your revision, I should pay particular attention to the following subjects – have you all got your pencils and notebooks ready?'... It is not my habitual modesty that makes me attribute my mark of 73 out of 75 to the qualities of my teacher. If he had still been in action, I think he might have appreciated the merits of performance-related pay.

An officer training establishment of this kind might reasonably have been expected to be ultra-pusser. We were certainly expected to behave smartly on parade and, as always, we had to spend a fair amount of our time ordering arms from the slope and performing similar evolutions with rifles; but on the whole the atmosphere was relaxed and most of the emphasis was on the acquisition of useful knowledge, rather than on appearances. A great deal depended on one's divisional officer, the man in charge of each weekly intake of about a hundred men. We were exceptionally lucky in being entrusted to Lieutenant Coldwell, the least pusser RN officer whom I encountered during the war. I have a happy memory of him running a negligent hand through his abundant golden tresses while reading out to us an instruction on the dire penalties awaiting those who failed to keep their hair cut short. When an earnest cadet enquired what he ought to do if he came across a couple of stokers fighting, Lieutenant Coldwell considered for a moment and replied gravely, 'If I were you I'd put my money on the bigger of them.' He gave me 21 marks out of 20 for an answer to a pilotage question since I thought of a highly improbable explanation that had not occurred to him.

Lieutenant Coldwell added to his many other virtues the fact that he was another would-be poet, who was trying to put together an anthology of naval verse. I naturally responded to his advertisement for contributions and this led to our spending a good many hours together, discussing each other's work and talking about literary matters in general. Differences of rank were forgotten; we were simply two friends arguing about civilized matters of interest to us both. Had I known that he would be required to recommend me for a particular kind of ship I feel sure that he could have been persuaded to endorse my own preference for something very small. I put in a request for something along those lines myself, but of course no one was going to pay any attention to that.

The general atmosphere reminded me of a junior common room. One of my friends overheard a conversation between two of our fellow cadets who were rolling back one evening, rather the worse for drink.

'All I ask is a tall ship and a star to steer her by.'

'You wouldn't know which one it was.'

'Never mind; I could still steer by the bastard couldn't I?'

If one was only entitled to one's ration of good luck, I was running through mine at a rather alarming rate. Before leaving Lancing for Hove, each division had to put on a revue. One of the highlights of ours was a silent version of the balcony scene in *Romeo and Juliet* in which Romeo produced an interrogative pendant and Juliet replied with an affirmative one.

Back in Hove for our last fortnight, we were accommodated in what was presumably a car park, underneath the municipal swimming pool. If I remember correctly, we were back in hammocks, perhaps because underground car parks are better equipped with stanchions than with bunks. Most of our time was taken up by examinations. I felt reasonably confident about navigation, pilotage and seamanship; and with the kind of helpful instructors that we had, failure in gunnery and torpedoes would have been the equivalent of a self-inflicted wound. That left signals and, of course, 'field training'. Try as I could, I was too slow to read any kind of visual, Morse or semaphore signal. By the time I had remembered what dash-dot-dot was meant to signify, I had missed the next three letters. But the comradeship of the sea is not entirely a myth; war is a collective effort and kind friends helped to pull me through. That left 'field training', at which I was always a poor performer. When the fatal day came, each of us took a turn at drilling the others and when I had to do my stint, everything worked like a dream, even though I was given one of the more treacherous manoeuvres – piling arms. My relief at this untypical proficiency was somewhat marred by the rumour that our instructor had awarded all the marks on the night before the examination, but I still passed. I don't remember anyone failing the examination as a whole – they must have been rather short of officers at the time. How well one did tended to reflect the time that had elapsed since one completed one's full-time education, so I emerged quite creditably.

The next scene was both painful and humiliating, as we struggled to get into our new uniforms. Whether because we wanted to look pusser, or because we had no alternative sources of supply, we had all equipped ourselves with starched collars that seemed to be made of armour plate. Trying to force front and back studs through these reduced us all to a state of writhing paralysis and the car park began to look like a collection of studies for someone's demented tableau of Laocoön. There were unsuspected problems concerning commissioned rank about which we ought to have been warned.

Resplendent in our bright new golden rings (since I was under twenty-one I was only a temporary *acting* sub-lieutenant, but it didn't show) we were sent off for a fortnight at Greenwich, to acquire a little social polish. There was not much work to be done, plenty of free time in London and the food was a cut above what my old Oxford college had been able to offer. The teaching was now mostly about how ships were run. I hope it is not merely my ignorance of the other two services that leads me to believe that junior naval officers have more to learn. A warship at sea is a self-contained unit; you cannot ring up headquarters for advice or instructions. Even a corvette is full of gadgets, quite apart from the guns and engines. It is also a community of rather a lot of people, who have to be administered and ought to be cared for. As officer of the watch at sea, or officer of the day in harbour, you are temporarily responsible for both ship and crew, and not merely in charge of your own particular department. Even after three months' training you know a good deal less about radar or torpedoes than the petty officers under your command, and everything seems to work by electricity. I was to spend a good deal of the next year hoping that no crisis would blow up that would expose my inability to cope with it, and suspecting that it was merely a matter of time before one did. That was for the future. For the time being we were not responsible for anything and all we had to do was to pick up a general familiarity with the shape of things, even if we had no practical knowledge of their content.

In the meantime we were magnificent in our shining new uniforms. I told my parents that if Churchill and I were to walk arm in arm down the Strand, people would be asking who he was. The first person who ever saluted me was a midshipman. I had my arms full of parcels and a pipe in my mouth and he only did it to embarrass me, but it was still a salute.

Not Really What You'd Call a War

I was in no hurry to exchange my temporary security for the Great Unknown and I thought that I had better acquire as much information as I could before confronting situations in which I would be assumed to know everything, so I put my name down for short courses in navigation and anti-submarine warfare. The first of these saw me back in Hove in mid-August, this time in luxurious accommodation in a rather good hotel, which I shared with Dennis Moore, my friend and companion from *Collingwood* and *Carnation*. We learned how to take sun and star sights. The theory of it was far beyond me – 'additional maths' in my School Certificate had not prepared me to cope with creatures like log haversines – but I became reasonably proficient in the practice. On the only occasion when I tried to use this knowledge I was severely reprimanded by the captain for taking a sun sight while on watch.

After yet another short leave I went up to Scotland towards the middle of October, for my asdic course. This time we were billeted on an antique Channel steamer and we did our sea training on what had once been a steam yacht. My fellow trainees were congenial enough and we were treated with courtesy and consideration but Campbeltown was rather different from Hove. It had been built for use rather than for pleasure and there was a greyness about everything that was an anticipation of what was to come. It rained most of the time. Local cultural facilities were not quite up to those in London but they were not entirely negligible. Campbeltown in those days boasted two cinemas, which were engaged in cut-throat competition. Each of them showed three different films every week, so, if we had nothing better to do, we could see a different film every night … except, of course, for the Sabbath. That was observed with true Calvinist rigour. One of the officers attached to the base (I seem to remember that he too was called Hampson) was so ill-advised as to try to do some gardening on a Sunday afternoon. No one said anything but his house was on a corner site and a small crowd of silent censors stood around on three sides and stared at him until their moral pressure sent him indoors.

Towards the end of the course I learned that I had been appointed to a Hunt class destroyer. That was a disappointment; I had asked for an anti-submarine trawler, since I suspected that any kind of a destroyer was liable to be pusser. I may have been ignorant and inexperienced but I knew what was good for me. A minor consolation was the fact that my destroyer was still being built, which might give me some time to learn the ropes or rather, the electrical circuits before we had to face the elements and the enemy.

My transition from lower deck to wardroom is perhaps as good a place as any for me to say a word about my attitude towards the conflict in which I was playing so inconspicuous a part. At no time did it ever occur to me that Britain might lose the war, which was an indication of credulity rather than of judgement. I was, after all, a trainee historian and I knew the way these things worked. I tended to take my bearings from the Napoleonic wars, which were more familiar to me than the 1914 conflict. 'We' began a major war with unsatisfactory allies. When these had been knocked out we carried on alone until the mistakes of the enemy provided us with more effective partners, with whose help we went on to finish the job. Eventual

My Hunt class destroyer.

victory being assured, my problem was to identify the stage that we had reached. We had obviously got beyond 1805 but I could not feel sure that we had reached 1812. The difference of a few years might not look all that important to the historian but things assumed another perspective when my own immediate future was involved.

I had no worries about the eventual defeat of the enemy but I was inclined to be pessimistic about what would follow. I had no confidence in the ability of any foreseeable British government to take advantage of the opportunity to build a better world, and grave reservations about the quality of the press, and even of the BBC. I was to change my opinion about the BBC a couple of years later when I heard over and over again how much it had meant to the people locked up in occupied France. My pessimism was not entirely to be blamed on my naïve and woolly attitude towards twentieth century politics. I heard during the summer of 1942 that the Commander-in-Chief of home forces had banned a poster urging people to 'Look ahead in war and plan for peace' on the grounds that it might distract the attention of the troops from the war effort. If that was the sort of thing that 'they' were saying now, it did not augur very well for the future.

I had arrived at the conclusion that the nineteenth century had been, on the whole, a progressive period, characterized by the growth of liberalism and humanitarianism. This had been brought to an end by the anarchic acceleration of industrialization and the evolution of unbridled capitalism. Technological change had become too rapid for politics to keep it under control. This meant that the new technological age had only two political options: 'fascism' and 'socialism'. Traditional conservatism, as exemplified by Neville Chamberlain, was inclined to lean towards the former. 'Appeasement' had signified, not so much peace at any price as a positive sympathy for any regime, however militaristic and totalitarian, that would 'keep the Russians out of Europe'.

I knew very little about the Soviet Union, but that was quite enough to convince me that Stalin had no respect for political liberty or human rights. Russia was, however, 'socialist', which meant that there must be hope of improvement there, whereas there was nothing at all to be expected from those who were leaning towards the 'fascist' side. Stalin might come to see the error of his ways, after his country had been regenerated by its 'patriotic' war. If not, there was always the hope that his successor might be a 'real socialist'.

This jumble of ignorance and prejudice makes strange reading fifty years later, but I suspect that it reflected a fairly general, if foggy, attitude amongst those who liked to think of themselves as progressive. I rarely mentioned Roosevelt when I was holding forth to my parents, but I think I regarded him as a kind of honorary socialist. I certainly thought that there was more to be expected from people like him, and perhaps from a reformed Stalin, than from die-hards like Churchill, who had been magnificent in 1940 but were too set in the old ways to be entrusted with building a new world. I had arrived at this curious jumble of opinions before I joined the navy, but in a vague sort of way it bore some relationship to the attitudes that I had encountered on the lower deck. It did not have much in common with those of the wardroom.

I left Campbeltown for yet another week at home, thoroughly spoiled by frequent leave and ample opportunities to make the most of the opportunities of London and to wander about the Sussex countryside, writing poems and sketching ruined abbeys. These had not exactly been 'days of philandering', but in all other respects, Figaro's aria to *Cherubino* was only too apposite. On October 29 I departed for England, home and disillusionment.

CHAPTER 4

WORKING UP

It all began pleasantly enough. Early in November I went down to Cowes to look for my ship. In the street I ran into my new commanding officer, who was out with the gunner. They directed me to the *Horse and Groom*, which served as our base for the next few days. It was rather like something out of *Treasure Island*. I took to the captain at once. He was friendly, cheerful and informal. 'Guns', who had risen from the lower deck, was a kind of up-market version of Wiggy Bennett (the petty officer in charge of our hut at HMS *Collingwood*). We seemed to be off to a good start.

By the middle of the month we had moved on board, where we were joined by the rest of the crew. As a divisional officer, I found myself directly responsible for the welfare of some of them. When one of 'my' seamen asked for compassionate leave to visit his sick baby, I commended his case to the captain and he was on his way home within twenty-four hours. This confirmed my belief that I was lucky in my commanding officer. The first lieutenant seemed to be a very different kind of man. He was efficiency personified but that appeared to be all there was to him and he lived entirely for his job. I wrote him off as the worst kind of RN officer – blinkered, arrogant and a mere fighting machine. The other watchkeeping officers consisted of two sub-lieutenants, one RN. and the other RNVR, not much older than me but more experienced, together with the amiable gunner. The wardroom was completed by the engineer officer, an Ulsterman of the less flexible kind, and the doctor. I took immediately to 'Doc', who combined the classless informality of his Canadian up-bringing with a cheerful humanity that was all his own.

During the next couple of months we spent a fair amount of our time at sea, either exercising or on passage, and I was able to observe my fellow officers on the job, which led me to revise some of my impressions quite considerably.

I came to the conclusion that the captain, for whatever reasons of personal choice or parental persuasion, was in a job for which nature had not intended him. His inclination to be affable and easy-going was at odds with the kind of authority that he had been trained to think that he ought to exercise, and as soon as he was at sea he became an entirely different man. I think he may have suffered from a kind of permanent identity crisis, convinced of the merits of strong and confident leadership without having the qualities that would have allowed him to exercise them. I diagnosed him at the time as 'a tin god with an inferiority complex'. If things did not work out as he would have wished, he took it for granted that this was due to the incompetence of his subordinates – but that was an attitude shared by a good many RN officers. His indecision and unsureness of himself, combined with his conviction that, as commanding officer, he knew better than everyone else, was expressed in bluster, sarcasm and the violent abuse of everyone around him. As the most junior officer on board, I came in for a particularly generous share of this.

One quality that the captain certainly did not lack was fighting spirit. He was the only sea-going officer or rating whom I encountered during the war who actually welcomed the prospect of what he liked to refer to as 'bloody battles'. That presumably reflected his training. He still deserves credit for his courage, but his way of expressing it made no converts. Everyone else preferred a quiet life. Our general distaste for 'bloody battles' was not diminished by our suspicion that if we got involved in one, the captain could be relied on to do something foolish.

One of the more irritating forms taken by his lack of self-confidence was his inability to delegate responsibility or to trust anyone to do a job satisfactorily. This applied to all his officers, but especially to me as the least experienced. I was particularly vulnerable since I shared a watch with the first lieutenant. The captain would quite frequently come on the bridge and offer to take No. 1's place, so that he could look after the general running of the ship. Sharing a watch with the captain was bad for one's blood pressure. From time to time he would tell me to check our position. This was quite important since we understood that coastal waters were protected by minefields, which would be inconvenient if we strayed outside the swept channel. 'Taking a fix' was one of the things that I had retained from my training course. It was not difficult and it was well within my competence, but the captain never allowed me to finish the job. While I was transcribing the bearings on to the chart a sharp elbow in my ribs would shove me silently out of the way and the captain did it himself. It happened like that every time and it was not a good way to train junior officers. When I had become familiar with the routine I naturally did not bother much about taking careful bearings, but simply went through the motions, since I was certain that I should be elbowed aside before I could do anything with my information.

His training at Dartmouth had taught the captain a great deal about warships and virtually nothing about anything else. One day, when chatting with the doctor and myself, he asserted that the man who had invented radar was the greatest genius who had ever lived. With all the brashness of my immaturity, I had no more sense than to reply that there had been one or two quite bright people in the past, like Leonardo da Vinci, for example.

'Who the devil's he?'

'You know, the man who painted the Mona Lisa.'

'What the hell are you blathering about?'

I was lucky. I tremble to think what might have happened if he had realized that I was referring to someone whom he would have regarded as a 'wop'. When the wind was in the right quarter, he could appreciate that there were more things in heaven and earth than appeared in the Dartmouth curriculum. On Christmas Day, when we were chatting in the wardroom, he profoundly shocked the engineer officer by suggesting that a naval education was regrettably narrow. 'Chief' insisted, on the contrary, that the navy was Britain's finest university. That made sense, from his point of view, since anything that was not wholly concerned with the senior service was unworthy of anyone's serious attention. The captain tried to bring me into the argument but for once I had the sense to keep out. Such occasional doubts, when they occurred to the captain, had to contend with his habitual conviction that, since he was the senior officer, he must be the ultimate authority on every subject that did not fall within the competence of a specialist branch, such as medicine or engineering. Once we were on active service he had to make important decisions and I suspected that his unacknowledged doubts about his omniscience made him all the more forceful in his assertion of it.

One result of all this was a particularly virulent strain of pusserdom. He once reprimanded me for saying 'Please' when, in harbour, I asked the yeoman of signals to bring me the signal log. 'In action you won't have time to say 'Please'. These men have to be trained in instant, automatic obedience.' When we *were* in action, being attacked by half a dozen torpedo-bombers, the captain, programmed by the formula he had used during countless hours of exercises, rattled off the wrong order. 'Alarm starboard, enemy in sight: aircraft, bearing green 150, angle of sight 05, *for exercise* open fire.' Putting in 'for exercise' meant that the guns would be trained in the appropriate direction but would only pretend to fire. The CW rating responsible for passing the order to the guns had been trained in instant obedience. He knew that it was the wrong order, and that it could even result in our being torpedoed, but it was not for him to exercise his own judgement and countermand his captain. He looked rather sad but said nothing. I savoured the irony of the situation for what seemed a long time and could well have been half a second, although I was as scared as the CW rating, before I deleted 'for exercise'. To do him justice, the captain later thanked me for this, but it did not lead him to revise his views about the merits of blind obedience.

As I suggested in a previous chapter, commanding officers tend to have very little contact with their crews, which is not a cause for much regret on either side. Our man seemed to have nothing but contempt for his, which is rather more serious. He once told me that their only reason for going ashore was to enjoy what he described as 'a quick poke'. He had no grounds for suspecting anything of the sort, but I could have assured him that the only reason his officers went ashore – in Malta, Tripoli or Alexandria – was to have a leisurely drink and exchange reminiscences about the navy, in some officers' club. That would have struck him as the only sensible way for them to spend their time.

The outcome of all this was that the captain led a kind of Jekyll and Hyde existence. After swearing at everyone on the bridge, when we got into harbour he would drop into the wardroom in a genial mood and expect all present to respond to his good humour. His RN officers seemed to find this normal and to have no difficulty in putting the recent sarcasm and insults to one side. My RNVR colleague, sub-lieutenant P, made himself as invisible as possible, but it was a game that I found myself unable to play. I suspect that I have always been rather prickly about my personal dignity and I resented being sworn at in front of the crew. The captain and I probably brought out the worst in each other.

If, in the remainder of this narrative, my attitude towards the more senior officers of the senior service is less respectful than might seem appropriate, I must ask the reader to make allowances for my own unfortunate experience. I am not trying to give an account of the navy during the second world war, but to describe what happened to me and how I reacted to it. There were no doubt many captains who combined fairness and efficiency with personal charm. Mine happened to be of a different kind. My own limited experience, over the next two or three years, led me to think that, although he may have been exceptionally trying, his behaviour was not wholly untypical of that of his tribe, but 1 was perhaps unfair in not making enough allowance for the element of stress in the exercise of command in wartime. In one of his more perceptive moods, when he must have recognized that I was exasperated by his behaviour, the captain once asked me if I thought that I would be capable of sailing the ship to America on my own. When I answered 'Yes sir,' he said 'I think you could, but you would find yourself under a lot of nervous strain.' It was a revealing comment. There were times when I got the impression that he was half aware of his unreasonableness but that didn't make any difference to his behaviour at sea.

My opinion of the first lieutenant changed equally radically, but in the opposite direction. He *was* a hard man, with an abrasive voice and a brusque manner that sounded offensive until you understood that it did not mean anything. In his own way he did his best for the crew – in things like getting them as much leave as possible – but he was a harsh disciplinarian who treated offenders as guilty until proved innocent and he was inclined to dismiss their explanations as so many lics. Slightly younger than the captain. his experience had been very different. He had joined the navy as a boy, to escape from the depression of the 1930s, and hated it ever since. He had fought his way grimly up to commissioned rank by hard work and professionalism. He knew his job inside out and he had an almost instinctive ability to do the right thing in a crisis. On a clear night in the Mediterranean when I was on watch with him, I looked out on the port beam and saw to my horror a stream of phosphorescent bubbles making straight for the ship at what I judged to be the speed of a torpedo. I was so startled that all I could do was grab his arm and shout 'Look!' Absolutely automatically he gave the appropriate wheel and engine orders and the ship was already beginning to respond when the dolphin reached it, dived under our keel and surfaced on the starboard side with a derisive snort. I have never been entirely convinced by the general tendency to regard dolphins as lovable creatures.

As the most junior watchkeeping officer, I was paired with the first lieutenant. Very much to my surprise, I found the experience most enjoyable. On the whole, he left the navigation to me. Once or twice during a watch he would say 'Where are we, pilot?' and I would take a fix and confirm that we were more or less in the middle of the swept channel. Since I had no desire to blow either of us up, I took my bearings carefully and he never checked them for himself. When a situation got rather too complicated and he could see that I was beginning to get out of my depth, he never got impatient or said 'Leave it to me.' He would discuss things from the perspective of a colleague who happened to have rather more experience, and unravel its complexities. I learned a great deal from him and we enjoyed being on watch together, provided that the captain stayed below.

No. 1, like the captain, was a lieutenant and he was inclined to resent the lack of consideration with which he was treated. It was his third posting as first lieutenant and, since I knew how good he was at his job, I could not help suspecting that his failure to obtain a command of his own was due to the fact that he had come up from the lower deck. He was recently married and his wife had her first baby about the time that we sailed for Scotland. That was what really interested him in life, although you had to know him well to discover it. He was not an amiable man and it was easy enough to see why the crew disliked him, but he was a man one could respect and whose leadership one would follow without hesitation. From time to time, when the captain had become more than usually insufferable, No. 1 would say wearily, 'I'll have to have a word with him' and depart for the captain's cabin. Raised voices would be heard and things would improve marginally for a day or two, but it never lasted.

I remember virtually nothing about the RN sub-lieutenant, although I have the impression that he was quite good at evasive action, where flak from the captain was concerned. Although he was an 'active service' officer – an odd way of referring to the people who manned the navy in peacetime – I have a hazy impression that he had not been given the full Dartmouth processing and that he did not feel entirely at home in any particular context. The other sub-lieutenant was an RNVR officer like myself. A teacher by profession, and the husband of a pregnant wife, for him the real world was something that existed outside the navy. He shared this attitude with the doctor and myself but he tended to keep out of the way and commune with himself. This was easier for him than for me since, as correspondence officer, he had a bunk in the ship's office. It was not something that you could dignify by the name of a proper cabin, but it was a bolt-hole of his own, somewhat off the beaten track; whereas the doll's house that I shared with the navigator and the gunner was just outside the wardroom. Once in foreign parts, Lieutenant P (as he had become) and I used to go exploring together and we got on very well, but the relationship took time to develop.

Where Doc, Guns and the engineer officer were concerned, experience confirmed and reinforced my initial impressions. Doc was all of a piece and the good-ness went all the way through. He took the view that the navy stopped at the door of his sick bay. On the other side there were neither admirals nor seamen but only patients, all of whom he treated in the same way. There was a swinging cot in that sick bay and it was usually occupied – not because of our high morbidity or Doc's excessive caution, but because he was a sociable man who liked having someone around with whom he could chat. He was, of course, in a privileged position; he was not expected to know anything about lowering sea boats or firing torpedoes and even our captain was not disposed to challenge his diagnoses. Quite rightly, the crew idolized him. When we censored their mail, he was the only officer they mentioned, and always with real affection. On things like that one can trust the opinion of the messdeck. From my own point of view, he was a beacon of warmth and sanity in a menacing world.

Guns was not in the same category where intellectual companionship was con-cerned, but he too was a great source of comfort. To think of him is automatically to add something like 'Bless his heart!' There was a Dickensian quality to him. Without anything to boast of in the way of looks, without pride or ambition, without rancour or a hard word for anyone, he went his cheerful way, taking everything in his stride and greeting each new disappointment or injustice with 'All these things are sent to try us.' He could never be an ally, but his warm-hearted solicitude was a source of comfort. He was a sort of honorary mother.

The engineer officer, like Doc, lived behind the security of his specialized knowl-edge. His sphere of influence did not impinge on that of the captain, who felt under no obligation, and indeed might even have felt it rather derogatory, to understand engines. This local omniscience fortified Chief in his satisfaction with his world and his place within it. He was fond of retailing the most hackneyed wartime clichés like 'The only good German is a dead German' as though he had just invented them. Ten years later he was probably saying the same thing about the Russians, with the same conviction. I felt that he would have regarded the suggestion that any of his opinions might be open to question as too absurd to merit serious discussion. When things were going well and you had had plenty of sleep, Chief's conviction of his infallibility about any subject under the sun could be reasonably entertaining. When you were living on your nerves to begin with, he was inclined to turn your thoughts towards justifiable homicide.

All of the RN officers were resolutely philistine. One would not expect a ward-room to sparkle with cultural or intellectual fireworks, but the total indifference of most of my fellow officers to anything outside the navy came as rather a shock. They had no interest whatever in any of the countries they visited and Lieutenant P and I were the only officers who ever went exploring. Any discussion of the nature or objectives of the war would presumably have been dismissed as 'politics'. The cap-tain once told me that he expected the next war to be against the Russians. This so exasperated me that I replied that I hoped not, since it might find us on opposite sides. I can understand why he must have found me rather trying.

My first disappointment came when we were allocated our duties. Despite my special courses in navigation and asdics, I found myself signal and torpedo officer, and confidential books and starshell control officer. Not entrusting me with navigating the ship was understandable enough, in view of my inexperience, but I knew even less about my new responsibilities. The starshell control business can be disposed of fairly briskly, since we fired starshell on only one occasion. That was when we were exercising off Iona. I remembered the correct orders and the first two stars floated gracefully down on their parachutes. When the guns fired for the third time nothing happened. 'The fool of a gunner' said the captain, 'has forgotten to fuse his starshell.' Next morning the 'fool of a gunner' checked his ammunition and discovered that he had one starshell too many and one high explosive shell too few. Whether we actually hit Iona or not, we never discovered, but I don't remember any reports of its suffering a naval bombardment.

As torpedo officer I was responsible, not merely for firing our two torpedoes, but for everything electrical throughout the ship. I was reasonably competent at mending a fuse but my electrical knowledge did not extend much further than that and I was at the mercy of my petty officers. Those in charge of radio and visual signals were thoroughly responsible and cooperative but in the torpedo petty officer I encountered another Sid (the rogue from HMS *Carnation*). He seemed to have a cousin, if not a wife, in every port, and he was always requesting permission to spend the night ashore. One day the engineer officer told me that there was not a single creda bar left in the ship's store. Not having any idea what they were, I did my best to express polite concern. He then explained to me that creda bars were what I knew as the 'elements' in electric fires, and that my benevolent petty officer had taken advantage of my readiness to sign anything he put before me to 'victual up' all his friends with their own electric fires. They had forgotten to tell us about creda bars during our training course.

Despite my outstanding performance in the torpedo examination, I did not feel any great confidence in my ability to fire the things in anger. The captain agreed with me that I needed to go on a course. So I left the ship, in Cowes, after an early breakfast, caught the ferry to the mainland and made my way to HMS *Vernon*, which is rather more widely known as Roedean Girls' School near Brighton. I completed my course and was back on board in time for dinner. Wartime 'courses' were sometimes more conspicuous for their intensity than for their duration. It was probably just as well that we were never called upon to fire our torpedoes either in practice or in anger. At least I could now include in my curriculum vitae, 'old boy of Lancing and Roedean'!

After various exercises, speed trials and the like, the ship was beginning to 'find herself', as Kipling would have put it. One day we rolled the knob off my cabin door and when we tried out our guns a whole door blew off. About the middle of December we set off to continue our training in Scottish waters. The weather was consistently foul. Our departure was delayed by a blizzard and there were gale warnings during three of our first four days at sea. To escape the weather, we were allowed a day's shelter at Dartmouth. When it was time to leave, the gunner earned himself a period of popularity by getting the after mooring rope entangled with the propeller, which gave us another day's peace until the divers could free it. Once at sea, the captain decided that since our main armament consisted of two sets of twin 4" guns, we would be divided into only two watches, so that one gun turret could be manned all the time. As a result, on one day I was on watch from 4 p.m. to 6, deciphered signals from 6 to 8, and was on watch again from 8 to 12 and from 4 to 8 a.m. Even he realized that we would not last very long at that rate and we reverted to the usual pattern of three watches.

The most important part of our final training took place at Tobermory, under the pitiless eye of the legendary Commodore Stephenson. He worked for 364 days of the year and we were there on the 365th – Christmas Day – when he organized a grand regatta to keep the crews from becoming bored. It was a very different Christmas from my previous one at Gibraltar. There were no decorations and no fraternization between wardroom and lower deck. This was an RN ship. What most distinguished her from *Carnation* was the sense of positive animosity between upper and lower decks. It was hard to believe that we were fighting the same war – for democracy, or so people said.

Commodore Stephenson presided over his own 'reign of terror'. One thing that our wardroom *did* have in common with *Carnation* was its weakness for a good rumour, the more macabre the better. It was reported that on one occasion Stephenson had removed all the officers from a ship he was inspecting, on grounds of incompetence. The grand finale of his training programme was a final explosion of controlled panic when an entire crew was confronted with a collection of imaginary crises. There was a story, which sounds much too good to be true, that on one of these occasions a ship's company had been reduced to a state of more or less demented chaos, with the single exception of a quartermaster who had nothing to do except stop strangers from coming on board. As he observed the surrounding pandemonium with a philosophical eye, Stephenson dashed up to him, flung his much-braided cap on the deck and shouted 'That's an incendiary bomb!', whereupon the quartermaster kicked it into the sea.

When our day of judgement came, I was detailed off to lower the dinghy. The problem here was that it nestled inside the considerably larger whaler and the falls (or lowering ropes), were designed for the whaler. If you fastened them to the dinghy you pulled the ends out of it. I had been taught how to cope with this during my training but it was one of the many things that I had forgotten. I was contemplating the problem when along came the captain, going at full speed round the ship, with Stephenson at his heels, trying to catch up with him and stop him telling people what to do.

'What are you doing?'

'Lowering the dinghy, sir.'

'Use the stretcher.'

Away he went, followed a few moments later by Stephenson.

'What are you doing?'

'Lowering the dinghy, sir.'

'How are you going to do that?'

'Use the stretcher, sir.'

'Stretcher's been shot away.'

He shot away too, in pursuit of the captain, who came round again, a minute or two later, on his second lap.

'Why aren't you using the stretcher?'

'Stretcher's been shot away, sir.'

'Put a tackle round the falls.'

Off he went again and it was Stephenson's turn.

'How are you going to launch that dinghy?'

'Put a tackle round the falls, sir.'

'And whose idea was that?'

As I remember it, he had a wart on his nose, with a long hair at the end of the wart, that he trained on his victims like a gun barrel. It was pointing at me now. I seemed to be hopelessly trapped between the devil and the deep brown wart. If I said that it had been my own idea, he would smell a rat and if he extracted a confession, I should be exposed as both incompetent and a liar. On the other hand, if I told the truth, I could look forward to an interesting session with the captain. It was desperation, rather than presence of mind, that prompted me to reply 'Not mine, sir.' Stephenson stood the wart at ease and looked at me with what was almost reluctant appreciation. 'Well, I suppose that's the second best answer you could have given me.' Away he pounded, after the vanishing captain, and that was that. I have no idea what he put in his report but he didn't take anyone off the ship.

Tobermory in wartime was scarcely a home from home, but we had not entirely severed our contacts with the civilian world. I was able to buy some excellent Scottish tweed as a belated Christmas present for my mother. The shopkeeper explained that of course he was not allowed to sell clothes, since they were 'on coupons' but that the fringes on his travelling rugs were easily detached and he had been told that they made good skirts.

As we exercised up and down off the coast, from time to time we caught tantalising glimpses of castles or country houses, half-hidden amongst the leafless trees. These excited me in a way that I had not known since I was a child and I came to the conclusion that what made things magical was their inaccessibility. The holiday motorist driving through the country can stop anywhere he likes and transform a flash of fairyland into yet another Victorian example of the Gothic revival. Children have to be content with the fleeting vision, and so had we, as we tested our star shell and depth charges and shelled Iona. Everything ashore was remote and unattainable, coexisting with our grey, metallic world, but aloof and unapproachable. When we moved to Scapa Flow, the strangeness shifted from buildings to the geography itself. Looking northwards, I felt that I could almost see the place where sky and water met, just over the horizon. Despite everything that I had learned on my navigation course, it was hard to resist the evidence of my own eyes that, if we were to sail that way, it would not be long before our masts got caught in the sky. Everything was slightly unreal and much of it was mysterious. I tried to express my feelings in a poem that I wrote at the time.

On passage

The thin rain falls all night; our wind-blown oilskins
Fondle the backs of our knees and the water trickles
Into our sodden sea-boots hour by hour.
We roll in a following sea and the masthead traces
Rainbows continually across the few wet stars.
As we slew to the galloping swell the solid water
Whitens beneath the bow and thunders onward.

Eastward the land stands dark above the water,
Where white lights wink all night from lonely headlands.
We keep the ramparts of this sleeping island,
Remote in wastes of time no less than water.

That coast throws pictures at our passing fancies,
Romantic place-names where the fairies linger,
The hall-sung territory of myth and saga.
Aloof in space and time, the barge of Arthur
Wailing to Avalon, the sunken city,
Is nearer than night-shifts, the tube, the seven-thirty,
Real as our sleeping homes, themselves now mythical.

All questions here have answers, all men's lives
Refocus as we breathe; in our hearts
Our heroes live; time's crazy carousel
Carries us with it and our place is kept.
We know too much for hatred, pity and pride
Shine back at us from all the friendly stars.

In the meantime we had more practical matters to keep us occupied. The weather got worse and worse. Rounding the too-well-named Cape Wrath, we were running at the same speed as the sea. Since there was little or no movement of water past the rudder, the ship could not answer her helm and we broached to four times in one watch, rolling 40–45° in each direction. On another occasion a particularly vicious wave sent all the officers in the wardroom, together with their chairs, into a slithering mass on the deck, with a pot of apricot jam in the middle. Crews of small ships were given 'hard-lying money' to compensate for that sort of thing. As a rather large 'small' ship, we qualified for a half share of this. There were times when I thought we earned it.

One night, when we were lying at anchor in Scapa Flow and the sea was getting rougher all the time, the coxswain of the motor boat reported to me, as officer of the day, that he thought it was too dangerous to make any more trips ashore. I passed this on to the captain, who ordered me to hoist the motor boat on board. This was more easily said than done. The boat was pitching wildly, secured by a rope to the end of a projecting boom. The bowman, followed by the coxswain, crawled out along the boom, hauled the boat beneath it, and jumped down on to its canopy, somehow managing to avoid going over the side as they wriggled their way into the cockpit. When a stoker began to follow, the coxswain waved him back, saying that he knew how to work the engines himself. He managed to steer the boat under its falls and I mustered enough seamen to hoist it safely on board. We could easily have lost one or two men, for there would have been no hope for anyone in that dark and icy water; but our only casualty was my cap, which blew away during the proceedings. The captain congratulated me several times on getting the boat back on board, when all that I had done was give orders from the safety of the deck. It was the others who had taken all the risks, but I was getting used to the idea that praise and abuse bore no relationship to anyone's desserts.

It was not at all clear to me what purpose we were supposed to be serving at Scapa Flow. We escorted new capital ships when they went out on gunnery practice, but since they were faster than us, they had to reduce speed so that we could keep up with them! By mid-January 1943 we knew that we were destined for the Mediterranean unless someone changed his mind. By the end of the month we were in Greenock. Everyone got three days' leave, which was just long enough for me to get home on what I suspected would be my last visit for a long time. My memories of Greenock are all grey; grey rain falling on grey buildings out of a grey sky; grey ships moving up and down a grey river. The news was rather grey too. To his undisguised joy, Doc was recalled to barracks. We did not begrudge him his release to a sphere where more people would be able to benefit from his warmth and humanity, but it was a cruel loss to us. His replacement was pleasant enough but tended to keep to himself and I never established with him the close relationship that I had had with Doc. Guns left us too, which deprived me of a cheerful companion, if not of a soul-mate. His replacement was much younger and briskly orthodox. My only refuge from pusserdom was now Lieutenant P, with whom I had not yet established much contact.

Not Really What You'd Call a War

Change was not entirely for the worse. A new RN officer relieved me of my responsibility for the torpedoes and for all things electrical. To compensate for this, I was put in charge of the plot, which had all the fascination of a complicated electronic game. It was situated in the wheelhouse, which meant that my anti-submarine action station would be warm, dry and so sheltered that I would be able to smoke my pipe even at night. I should also be well out of the captain's way. The plot consisted of a mechanical device that translated the ship's movements on to a spot of light on a large sheet of paper. When hunting a submarine, one marked in one's own position and that of the submarine, as recorded by the ship's asdic. In this way one was soon in a position to make a reasonably accurate estimate of its course and speed. I had done this many times during anti-submarine exercises ashore, where the plot tended to be dismissed as of very minor importance. I took a more optimistic view of its possibilities. Since asdic operators were liable to lose contact with their targets, the man on the plot often had the best overall view of what was going on and he could direct them back on to their target. Besides, it really *was* very peaceful in that wheelhouse. Once in the Mediterranean, aircraft were more of a problem than submarines. This was inconvenient. There was nothing for me to do in the event of an air attack, so the captain decided that I might as well hang about the bridge and relay his orders to the guns. I soon came to understand that courage is largely a matter of having plenty to keep you busy. When we were in action against a submarine, it did not occur to me that this was any different from our exercises off Tobermory and that this one might bite. Air attacks were a very different matter, since all I had to do was to watch the enemy coming at us. That petrified – or, to be more accurate, jellified me. In a desperate effort to find something to do and to get back to the wheelhouse, I got hold of a sheet of transparent plastic and some chinagraph pencils and tried to persuade the captain that I could handle the incoming information from our radar quickly enough to plot the course of the enemy aircraft and get the guns pointing more or less in the right direction before an attack developed. I don't blame him for being sceptical since my information would only be really valuable after nightfall and the enemy didn't do much bombing after dark. My motives were both suspect and disingenuous, but I believe they operated the kind of anti-aircraft plot that I was suggesting in one or two big ships, and I still think that it was workable. It was not to be, and I remained on the bridge and tried to keep my knees as stiff as possible.

All that was for the future. I could now look forward to some real active service, in a job where the inadequacy of my knowledge was liable to catch me out at any time, without a friend on board to whom I felt attached, and under the orders of a captain who had already demonstrated his ability to make life very unpleasant when we were at sea. I told my parents and I tried to convince myself, that things were bound to improve, but I had no reason to believe that they would.

CHAPTER 5

ACTIVE SERVICE

We left Greenock about the 7th of February 1943, taking our usual weather with us as far as Milford Haven, where it blew a force 12 gale. We kept anchor watches all night and hoped that the weather would be too bad for our convoy to put to sea. We were disappointed as usual and on the next day we sailed to join half a dozen merchant ships that were carrying troops to Algeria, which allied forces had occupied three months earlier. We carried two passengers with us, a man from the Foreign Office, who had known W.H. Auden when they were both undergraduates at Christ Church, and an ebullient journalist (described by the captain as 'the Jew boy') who claimed to have worked for the *Manchester Guardian* and was now some kind of naval press officer. They provided some temporary consolation for the loss of Doc and Guns and gave me a chance to talk about something other than the navy.

I was now introduced to another of the mysteries of my trade, the art of station-keeping. Convoy and escort zig-zagged together, to make life more difficult for possible submarines, with the warships throwing an asdic screen around the merchantmen. To do this efficiently, each of them had to maintain its appropriate position, in terms of range and bearing, in relation to both the convoy and the other escorts. Unless one went about it the right way, correcting a fault in either was liable to induce one in the other. With the help and encouragement of the first lieutenant I soon became reasonably proficient at this not very difficult art. Problems arose when another escort vessel was badly out of its own station. One then had the choice between keeping station on the escort or retaining one's correct position with regard to the convoy and disregarding the aberrant behaviour of the other warship. Either alternative was calculated to weaken or displace the pattern of the asdic screen. Whichever solution we adopted, the captain, if he happened to be on the bridge, reprimanded us for not having chosen the other. When we requested him to tell us which course of action he wanted us to adopt, he replied that it was a question of exercising our tactical judgement. That meant that we were sure to get it wrong every time.

The same kind of problem was continually recurring in one way or another. During one of my watches when I was on the bridge with the captain, a lookout reported a packing case floating in the water ahead of us. Since we were not going to collide with it, I replied 'Very good' and continued on my course. This provoked an outbreak from the captain. 'What the hell do you mean, "Very good"? You've no idea what may be in that case. Go and pick it up.' So I altered course and we hauled the case on board. Soon afterwards the lookout spotted another one. By this time I felt that I knew the drill and I immediately ordered 'Port fifteen'. This made the captain even more abusive. 'What the hell are you doing? Do you think this is a bloody shit cart? Get on your way.'

I have always been inclined to think of *Catch 22* as a realistic war novel. Perhaps I should have taken this kind of thing philosophically, but to be sworn at in public is never very pleasant. Over the next six months we were going to be at sea almost all the time, which meant that we were continually short of sleep and being abused today for doing what one had been insulted for not doing the day before could become very wearing.

We delivered our convoy at Oran and left almost at once for Algiers. On the way there we spent three hours attacking an asdic contact that may have been a submarine. We failed to hit anything, eventually gave up the chase and continued on our way, now somewhat short of depth charges. When we reached Algiers we were ordered out again the same evening, without having had a chance to reload, together with another destroyer, to hunt for a second submarine that had been sighted on the surface.

We seemed to have missed that one but at three in the morning we encountered another, which submerged as soon as it sighted us. The two destroyers then carried out a number of depth charge attacks and I was busy on the plot, recording our movements and trying to estimate those of the submarine. At least we knew that, this time, there actually was one. By about half-past six we seemed to be getting nowhere and we had lost asdic contact with our target. I suggested to the captain that the submarine seemed to be trying to escape to the north and that if it managed to get clear it might surface and make off at speed. I therefore proposed that we should make a northerly sweep in order to counter any possible manoeuvre of that kind. I think that was the only time that he ever took any notice of my opinion, and it almost lost us our submarine.

Eventually we returned from our sweep, without making radar contact with anything, and had to start all over again. The captain then asked me the last reported bearing of the submarine from the position to which we had returned. This was a little tricky, since I had had to change the scale of the plot when we charged off on our northern excursion, but I managed to work out a 30° arc for our asdic sweep. The asdic operator picked up an echo at once which he failed to notice. He was subsequently awarded a mention in despatches. The officer of the watch, who detected the echo on the bridge loudspeaker, and told him to investigate it, got nothing.

We were now in contact again and for the next couple of hours both destroyers made a number of ineffectual attacks. From my position on the plot I could see that we were making the usual mistake of dropping our depth charges astern of the target. Our last attack was much better – we were told afterwards that it had sent a jet of water through the boat – but by this time we had fortunately only two depth charges left, so we did not do it any serious damage. Our partner had almost exhausted his supplies too, so we found ourselves in the absurd position of sitting on top of a submarine without being able to do anything more effective than to say rude things about it. Commodore Stephenson would not have been proud of us.

The Italians, however, had no means of knowing how harmless we were and, understandably, they had had enough. About nine o'clock the submarine surfaced, within a quarter of a mile of us. After a minute or two her crew came out on deck, she began to sink and they took to the water. Our captain then signalled to the other destroyer, 'I suggest we leave them.'

I was utterly horrified. He did not even have the miserable pretext of wanting to avenge our casualties since the submarine had not done either of us any harm. I know what I ought to have done. I knew it at the time and I am ashamed of myself for not having done it, but it is not easy to tell a captain, on his own bridge, what he is not allowed to do. I tried to ease my conscience by promising myself to request a transfer as soon as we returned to harbour and, if necessary, giving my reason. Mercifully, the captain of the other destroyer, a lieutenant-commander RNVR was senior to our man and he replied 'Lower your boat'. We did not go so far as that, but we hung out scrambling netting over the side and, as I understood, picked up all but five of the submarine's crew of fifty-two. At least I had not become an accessory to a war crime. Since my rather difficult objective was to help to win the war without doing anything to kill anybody, this could be considered at least a partial success. I tried not to think of those other five.

The captain, who was to get another medal, presumably for perseverance, congratulated me very warmly for my work on the plot. I calculated that that should insure me against his customary abuse for at least twenty-four hours, but I am always inclined to be optimistic.

When the Italian engineer officer climbed on board he said 'Now I learn English.' I heard that he had a close relative in Algiers and that he was looking forward to seeing her again. The submarine commander told our captain that he had no great objection to becoming a prisoner of war. 'I know you don't hate the Italians. You hate the Germans but my God, you don't hate them as much as we do.' If he had known about that infamous signal, he might have felt rather differently. Months later, one of the Italian crew wrote a rather fine letter to Lieutenant P. I said that I was going to reply to him but I can't remember whether or not I did.

Once the *Asteria* had surfaced, my job on the plot was over and I exchanged my pencils for my camera. I got exactly the kind of photographs that the press wanted, one of the submarine on the surface, with her crew on the deck, and the other of

The Asteria; Mediterranean, 1942.

her stern disappearing, with the sailors in the water. The journalist whom we had taken out to Algiers, excited by the exploit of 'his' ship, probably pulled a few strings to publicize our somewhat less than heroic feat of arms and my photographs appeared in most of the national newspapers, together with more or less misleading accounts of what had happened. My favourite was the one that described the submarine as having been sunk by gunfire, when a glance at the picture showed that she was undamaged. My pictorial contribution to the allied war effort brought me an unexpected £40, which may not seem much today, but worked out at more than two months' pay. In my humble way, I may have been responsible for a change in Admiralty policy. Not long afterwards Their Lordships decreed that the maximum that anyone in the navy would be allowed to earn from a negative was £5. Presumably the navy was going to pocket the rest. If they thought that this would guarantee them a steady flow of pictures they were perhaps being optimistic.

After a day at Algiers, where we replenished our supply of depth charges, we took a convoy to Bône, where we were able to go ashore for the first time. Lieutenant P and I undertook the first of our historical expeditions, to the extensive remains of the city of St. Augustine. A surly custodian told us that we were not allowed to see the site because it was dangerous. When we pointed out to him that several groups of people were going round, he suddenly became the soul of affability, welcomed us in and offered to trade his stock of minor finds for cigarettes. When we went back on the following day he treated us to exactly the same performance.

Back in Algiers, we made the most of the local facilities. These provided the context for our most enjoyable evening on board. The captain was dining in the wardroom, as he always did when we were in harbour. On that occasion he had invited an RN friend of his, with whom to share reminiscences, The friend looked and behaved as though he was giving an over-enthusiastic performance as Sir Andrew Aguecheek. His rather vacuous face was adorned with a blond moustache of improbable length. One end curled upwards in a rather dashing way. The other one drooped. Most of us had been ashore and we were not used to the local wine, which made up in potency for what it lacked in refinement. Whenever we glanced at Sir Andrew and his facial eccentricity, we could not refrain from a giggle. The captain glowered but had to pretend to be unaware of our deplorable manners as he went on grimly with his reminiscences. It was not much of a compensation for all that he made us suffer, but it was better than nothing.

The beginning of March saw us back in Bône, preparing to leave for a secret destination. We loaded up with miscellaneous trade goods, such as sacks of signal codes and a couple of torpedoes that we had to stow on the upper deck - the first lieutenant said that they were going over the side at the first hint of action. When a wrapper came off one of the parcels of signal codes we all knew that we were destined for Malta. After the French armistice in 1940, heavy naval losses had obliged the Admiralty to abandon convoys through the Mediterranean. We and another Hunt class destroyer were the first ships to go through for quite some time. We therefore found ourselves in the rather bizarre situation of being provided with an escort of two heavy fleet destroyers to protect us as far as the Sicilian Narrows.

Soon after the fleet destroyers turned back, the Italians suddenly switched on a lighthouse, which was disconcerting, since they were presumably not doing it to help us with our navigation. We heard afterwards (one always tended to hear an explanation for everything, sooner or later, without any means of verifying it) that they were sending a convoy round the south of the island. By 3.30 we were within eight miles of the coast ourselves. We carried two sets of radar, one for general purposes and another, more precise, but also more temperamental, for directing the guns. The latter was in one of its moods and it began picking up echoes from every point of the compass. This led the captain to believe, or at least to contemplate the possibility, that we were surrounded by enemy motor torpedo boats. He may only have been doing it to annoy, but when he began talking of firing his 'pieces' at these imaginary targets – and giving away our position to all and sundry – we became seriously alarmed. I kept repeating that the other radar set was not reporting any echoes and he eventually left things alone. That sort of thing was to happen on another occasion. I think he liked to imagine himself dashing into action, even when he knew that it would be liable to be suicidal. It was a relief when dawn came, bringing with it a Spitfire escort, and we entered Malta without incident.

Here we spent a few days, which allowed Lieutenant P and me to resume our historical wanderings although, without any transport, we were confined to Valetta. As a trainee historian, I had been inclined to adopt a rather patronizing attitude towards the Knights of St. John. That changed rather abruptly when I was confronted with the scale and complexity of their fortifications. The wartime economy of Malta was somewhat eccentric. You could buy films, but only if you also bought a camera with each one! The currency consisted of British pennies and Maltese notes for shillings. Things like boat trips back to the ship were very cheap … but no one ever had any pennies so, in practice, nothing cost less than a shilling. At least the natives were friendly and enthusiastically pro-British, which was a contrast to the attitude that we were to find further east.

From Malta we took a convoy to Tobruk, where we were able to go ashore for an hour or two. I remember it as looking more like a battlefield than a base, with the wreckage of both land and sea warfare strewn all over the place. It was difficult for the non-military mind to understand why it had been so important. Somewhat later I heard the story of the Naval Officer in Charge at Tobruk who made a desperate signal to Alexandria, 'Am all alone and without food. 20,000 Australians have just landed. Request instructions,' to which he received the reply 'Avoid being eaten if possible. Help is coming'.

On our way back westward we experienced our first air attack, a combination of high level and dive bombing, with a little torpedo bombing thrown in for good measure. One stick of bombs fell quite close to us but there was no damage to either convoy or escort. We reached Tripoli safely and took no harm from a second air attack. The Tripoli barrage was famous for its intensity and on this occasion it opened up without any air raid warning, just as one of our boats' crews was scrambling back on board. There were so many shell splinters coming down that two of our seamen received minor injuries before they could get under cover. The BBC reported that three of the attacking aircraft had been shot down by HMS *Derwent*. None of us believed it but she was, after all, the flotilla leader.

The air raid of March 19 was a very different business. This time the bombers got in before the barrage opened up, and hit a couple of ships. One of these was a tanker, moored near the entrance to the harbour, and the other, berthed quite near to where we were lying at anchor, was said to be carrying thousand-pound bombs. After about half an hour the small arms ammunition in the second ship began exploding. There would be a bang, a whizz and a hiss, when a piece of hot metal hit the sea. I must confess to ducking behind the side of the bridge every time I heard a bang, without waiting for the whizz. As the fire gained ground, we could see a red glare through the perforated hull of the ship. The next thing to happen was the sound of a torpedo hitting HMS *Derwent*. Since it was now some time since the enemy aircraft had disappeared, we decided that this must be a one-man or human torpedo, despite the improbability of a perfectly synchronized air and torpedo attack. It was, in fact, a circling torpedo, dropped by one of the aircraft, that had been wandering round the harbour until it found *Derwent*.

For an hour or two nothing else happened. We had lined our deck with riflemen, to shoot at the non-existent one-man torpedoes. One of them got rather a shock when a metal fragment from the burning ship carved a gash in the rifle butt between his hands, but he escaped unhurt. I was on anchor watch, not long after midnight, when there was a noise like the end of the world, as the bombs in the ammunition ship all went up together. I found myself flat on my face beneath the chart table without any idea as to how I had got there. I crawled out with some apprehension and held a roll call to see which parts of me were missing. Rather to my surprise, I discovered that I was intact. Then I saw a pair of legs, also sticking out from under the chart table. Steeling myself for a gruesome spectacle, I pulled them out, together with the signalman to whom they belonged. He was in one piece too. Our total losses that night amounted to one damaged rifle butt, although that was not the impression one would have gained from the engineer officer's records. Ever since we left Britain he had been making a careful list of any items of equipment that had suffered from accidents and negligence of one kind and another. The amount of stuff that was now written off as 'damaged by enemy action' was a credit to the Luftwaffe.

When anything untoward happens, the officer of the watch should always inform the captain. I was perhaps not feeling at my best and it did not occur to me that, since the explosion must have been audible half way to Malta, he might have heard it for himself. I was trying to get him on the voice pipe when I discovered that he was standing by my side. We were told later that the engines of the shattered ship had gone right over our heads and come down in the town. That sounds rather unlikely, although we did find a few bits and pieces on the deck. It also rained on us for a few seconds. The vacuum caused by that mighty explosion must have drawn up part of the sea, some of which fell back on us. The ammunition ship had presumably been also carrying a certain amount of grain, which had got mixed up with the sea water, for when dawn came we found ourselves covered with cereals from masthead to deck, which made us look like some sort of an advertisement for corn flakes. Oil from the shattered bunkers of the ship had ignited and the flames were spreading slowly across the harbour in our direction. As we made our way out, we passed the tanker, which presented a curious spectacle. Her cargo was vaporizing, but its expansion drove out the air from the tanks and the lack of oxygen prevented the petrol vapour from igniting. It shot out of the ship's ventilators in an invisible stream, like steam from a kettle, caught fire after a few feet and blazed away like a blowlamp. We thought it wiser not to hang around to see whether or not anything was going to disturb this equilibrium.

A week later we were in Alexandria, where we were able to get ashore. Lieutenant P and I, of course, were itching to get away to Cairo, a mere three or four hours away, but the ship was at four hours' notice for steam and there was no prospect of extended leave. In the meantime we found compensation in Alexandria. In those days there were plenty of shops selling 'finds' from excavations – or perhaps loot – and I soon began to build up a little collection. There were also the piano concerts, given every week by a man called, I believe, Baron George Menasches, who generously threw open his home to any members of the forces. Any classical music that dared to trespass on the wardroom radiogram was immediately evicted, so Lieutenant P and I found the combination of good music, goodwill, elegant domestic surroundings and refreshingly unpusser food, irresistible. On our first visit, when he heard that we were going on to another concert at the YMCA, the baron gave us a lift in his luxurious car, which completed the Arabian Nights effect.

Getting back on board was quite an adventure in itself. The ship was moored far out in the bay and in order to make contact with our liberty boat we had somehow to pick the right landing stage from a maze of anonymous jetties. On one occasion, Lieutenant P and I were reduced to hitching a lift back on a tug. Once we got to know the ropes, we ignored the liberty boat and hired a felucca. One of my proudest wartime memories concerns one of these felucca trips. The boat that I had hired was swift and powerful and there was a strong breeze blowing. As usual, the boatman handed me the tiller – he was presumably calculating that, if I smashed up the boat, I should have to provide him with a new one. There was a passenger in our boat and the owner gave me to understand that he wanted to be put ashore at a particular jetty. Away we raced and then I threw the tiller over and for a second or two the felucca hung absolutely still, in the eye of the wind, a yard or so from the jetty. The passenger leapt ashore and with another flick of the tiller I sent us racing away before the wind. I am still wondering how I ever had the nerve to do it.

From Alexandria we went to Port Said for a boiler clean, which gave us a few days in harbour. Lieutenant P and I took advantage of the chance to get away from the ship and made a pleasant excursion down the Suez Canal to Ismaelia. The charms of Port Said were somewhat marred by the swarms of hawkers who gathered like flies as soon as one sat down for a drink. On one occasion, when the usual queue had formed, I bought a wallet from the first salesman, for the equivalent of 10p, and then tried to sell it to each of the others. Reactions varied. Some were furious and others thought it an immense joke. One of them settled down to a session of hard bargaining. Each of us was rather disorientated to be doing things the wrong way round – he trying to force me down and me trying to push him up. I did get him up as far as the purchase price, but I felt that the honour of the Empire required me to make a profit ... and so I brought the wallet back home at the end of the war.

Later on I was to see a good deal of Port Said. This experience gave me a certain advantage over transit passengers, where local commerce was concerned. I once bought a newspaper from a boy in the street. He began by offering me the previous day's paper. When I handed this back to him he substituted the correct one, quoting its price as ten piastres. I pointed to the printed price of five piastres. 'Five piastres in Cairo, ten piastres in Port Said.' So I returned the paper to him again. He then agreed to accept five piastres but unfortunately I had nothing less than a ten-piastre note, which allowed him to pretend to miscount my change. You could get most things in Port Said, and at a reasonable price... provided you were not in a hurry. A curious characteristic of Egyptian hawkers was their passion for a bet. Rather than sell you their Turkish delight, imitation leather wallet or collection of pornographic pictures (only the top one reliably so; the rest were usually views of the pyramids) for 50 piastres, they would much sooner toss you for 100 piastres or nothing, 90 or 10, 80 or 20. Their ability to make calculations of probability at high speed in a foreign language did credit to their intelligence.

Then we were off again, on a succession of trips to Alexandria, Tobruk, Tripoli and Malta, with no time for more than the occasional trip ashore on ship's business. One day in April, in the Gulf of Sirte, I turned to the first lieutenant when it came light and said 'This is my twenty-first birthday' and he said 'Have a cigarette'. That was the end of that particular celebration. On May 1 our convoy was shadowed by a couple of enemy aircraft, both of which were shot down, but not before they had reported back our position. At dusk we were the target of a well-co-ordinated assault by dive bombers and torpedo bombers. We seemed to be the main target of the dive bombers, which gave us plenty to occupy our attention. They straddled us with a stick of bombs but we were not hit. It was all over within twenty minutes and we sailed on into the night, unaware that a tanker and a troopship had been sunk, until we were ordered to go and look for survivors. It was said that most of the tanker's crew were saved but that there was heavy loss of life on board the troopship. This was the only convoy that I ever escorted in which any ships were sunk, and what was most striking was the unreality of it all. Preoccupied with our self-preservation, we never noticed what was going on around us. I cannot remember whether or not we fished any survivors out of the sea; if we did, I never saw any of them. When we heard that several hundred men had been lost from the troopship, it was as though the whole affair was something that we had heard over the radio. It was said that several of the torpedo bombers had been shot down but no one ever asked what had become of their crews. This was, of course, one of the reasons why I had opted for the navy: you didn't even see the men whom you killed, or who killed you. It was perhaps less brutalizing than close combat in the army, but it tended to leave you insensible, even if it did not make you sadistic.

The sequel to this attack revealed an unexpected side to the captain's character, that was in remarkable contrast to his everyday behaviour. Since this involved a question of discipline, I had better begin with a word about the administration of what passed for justice on board HM ships. Suspected offenders were first reported to the officer of the day, in theory for investigation, in practice almost always for punishment. Junior officers like myself were authorized to dismiss cases but not to impose penalties. We put people who were still suspect in the first lieutenant's report. At first lieutenant's defaulters, No. 1 was surrounded by all those officers who happened not to be otherwise engaged, to add solemnity to the ceremony. He could impose minor punishments himself but referred more serious cases to the captain's defaulters, where the same ceremony was repeated.

We had recently acquired a seaman whose previous ship had been sunk by bombing. His action station was on one of the gun platforms, which was as safe a place as any, if it came to going over the side, but he was suffering from what would have been known as 'shell shock' during the previous war. When the air attack began he ran and hid as far below the waterline as he could get, which kept him away from the noise but would not have done him any good if the ship had been hit. Deserting one's post in the face of the enemy was just about as heinous a crime as one could find in the naval penal code, and he naturally ended up in the captain's defaulters, where he pleaded guilty.

'I suppose you know that you could be shot for this?'

'Yes sir.'

'Well you'd better go and see a psychiatrist when we get to Alexandria. Case dismissed.'

If only he could have behaved like that in his conduct of day to day business, the ship would have been a very different place.

My experience in *Carnation* had not prepared me for defaulters' sessions, even if the crew had talked all the time about people being put 'in the rattle'. In this ship they were a regular recurrence, and a depressing one, as sullen ratings who had committed some trivial misdemeanour were made to feel like criminals, harangued and given an hour's extra work for two or three days. How this affected life on the messdeck I can't say but it must have made its contribution to all the other animosities that pusserdom provoked and then took for granted.

On the whole, 'defaulters' was a drearily predictable affair, but there were one or two exceptions. I had a brief moment of glory on the day at Greenock when I had returned from my leave and taken over as officer of the day. That evening about ten ratings were mustered in front of me, charged with being late back from leave. It was midwinter and in those days trains were occasionally late. The men in front of me had barely had time to visit their families and they knew that they would be unlikely to see them again for months or years. Their own lack of punctuality had not delayed anyone else from going on leave or involved any other inconvenience.

I knew the kind of language that was expected of me:-

'I'm not interested in your excuses. Are you late or not? You ought to have realized that train was liable to be struck by lightning and caught the one before, etc. etc.'.

I preached them a little sermon on the virtues of punctuality and dismissed the lot.

One day when I was on the bridge with the captain – which is becoming as much of a refrain as 'once upon a time…' – the leading steward came up and said that he wanted to report the wardroom steward for disobedience of orders. This was something very unusual, since offences of that kind were never dealt with at sea but were held over until we got into port. The captain, with suspicious casualness, told me that he would look after the ship while I dealt with the case. When challenged, the steward admitted that he had indeed disobeyed the order. When I asked him what it was, he replied 'Not to make so much fuss about serving the officers but just to slap it about.' It can't have been the first of April, since I know from my diary that we were in harbour all that day, and I had no idea what was going on or how I was expected to react. I gave each of them a little lecture, about the virtues of obedience and the crime of issuing seditious orders, and dismissed them both. The captain never asked me what had been going on, about which I suspected that he knew more than I did.

Perhaps the most entertaining *cause célèbre* was the 'Case of the Wardroom Mincer'. An engine room artificer was accused of stealing the mincer and returning it with a broken butterfly nut. This had presumably been brought before the officer of the day who, realizing its gravity, had referred it to the first lieutenant's report. No. 1, who was not qualified to deal with matters of such seriousness, had then referred it to the captain. When he appeared before this august tribunal, the accused denied having stolen the mincer, which he claimed that a wardroom steward had allowed him to borrow. The case was therefore adjourned. At the next sessions the wardroom steward confirmed that he had authorized the artificer to borrow the mincer, but not to break the nut. The accused denied having broken the nut and claimed that it had come apart in his hand. This produced another referral, for a technical report by the engineer officer on the state of the nut. Chief confirmed that there had indeed been a hairline crack in the nut but observed that, in his professional opinion, if used with care, the nut would not have come apart. The case being now concluded, the captain pronounced the artificer guilty, of careless damage if not of theft, and ordered him to repay the entire cost of the nut – I cannot now remember whether this was 3d or 6d. What impressed me most about the whole business was the fact that I was the only officer who seemed to see anything funny in it.

There were two escort groups working between Alexandria and Malta and we got the impression that if a load of mail arrived for us just after we had sailed from either terminus, it was sent off by the other group and the same thing happened again at the other end. In theory this meant that neither group would ever receive any mail, but from time to time someone would blunder and we would get half a dozen sacks of letters. I once received sixteen letters from home by the same post. Whenever the mail caught up with us the crew abandoned all thoughts of shore leave and got down to the business of writing replies. All these letters had to be censored and since there were over twenty ratings to every officer, we gathered round the wardroom table for some intensive reading.

Like most things on board, censorship posed unexpected problems. Their Lordships, in their wisdom, had decreed that one or two crosses at the end of a letter were to be regarded as expressions of endearment, but that any in excess of a specific number – which I have forgotten – were to be excised, on the suspicion that they constituted some sort of code. The difficulty here was that some of our more romantic correspondents embroidered every page of their letters with a kind of lacework pattern made up of literally hundreds of crosses, which produced the effect of a sort of Victorian valentine. If we cut out all of the offending symbols there would be nothing left to return to the envelope. We made a policy decision to allow these letters through, on the ground that neither the sender nor the recipient would be able to add up all the expressions of affection without losing count. Censorship had its compensations. A very popular member of the ship's company had the endearing habit of sending to his wife or girl friend a collection of the ruder cartoons that he had cut out of *Men Only*. They made a quick tour of the wardroom table before going back into their envelope.

The messdecks had a life of their own which, in spite of everything, must have been sweetened by some of the cheerful irreverence that I had enjoyed in *Carnation*, but this was something that I only glimpsed on rare occasions. Lieutenant P was rather better placed. His action station was in the 'director', a gunnery control position away from the bridge, where the captain could not hear what was going on. Once, when we were approaching Alexandria (and in safe enough waters for the Gunner and me to decide that it was a 'pyjama night') the captain concluded the daily ritual of dusk action stations with instructions to keep a particularly sharp lookout during the night since there was always the prospect of a submarine attack. We were within range of enemy motor torpedo boats and a sortie by the Italian fleet (whose nearest base was only about 750 miles away) was a possibility. The director's crew passed on this message to the guns in a somewhat amended form: 'From the captain, secure action stations; for the night, expect to meet: U-boats, E-boats, the Italian fleet, the German fleet, the Japanese fleet, and cavalry!'

On May 9 we were ordered to Malta to join the miscellaneous collection of ships that was preventing the remnants of Rommel's army from getting away from Tunisia. Elated by the prospect of bloody battles, the captain ordered me to pack up all our confidential books – the usual precaution when one was engaged in hazardous enterprises in enemy coastal waters and take them to the signal office ashore, without waiting for a formal order to do so. When I surprised those concerned by turning up with my sackfuls, they told me that what I should really be wanting was my camera. Everything that would float had been sent to sea, including a couple of cruisers that were such permanent residents of Valetta harbour that we suspected they might be stuck to the bottom. We were not used to keeping company with such mighty fighting units, and when we heard the BBC refer to them as 'our light forces' we wondered how they would have described us!

All that we saw of the Afrika Korps was a few boatloads of men waving white flags. Our only danger came from the RAF and the American Air Force, which were said to have bombed one or two ships under the impression that they were enemy rescue ships. Reading the situation report before we left Malta, I had noted with interest that there was a German gun battery on Cape Bon that was said to be 'shelling with accuracy' up to a range of five or six miles. Since our scheduled patrol was due to pass much closer than that, I hoped that allied troops would get there first. They didn't, but the German gunners opened fire too soon. They straddled us with their first salvo but we were soon out of their range. True to form, the captain talked of going back and risking losing his ship in order to have his bloody battle, even though he knew that the battery was due to be overrun within a few hours. He didn't do it and he may just have been putting on a show for our benefit, but we could never be sure.

During May and June we were almost continually at sea; during one period of 39 days we spent only one full day in harbour. To ease the strain we experimented with fixed watches. In the usual way, watches rotated, so that one was on watch from 8 p.m. to midnight, from midnight to 4 a.m. or from 4 a.m. to 8 on consecutive days. This allowed one decent night in three but prevented one's body from adjusting to any fixed routine and we thought it might prove less tiring if we did the same watch every night. The question was, of course, who was to get the 'middle' watch from midnight onwards and the answer was obvious. By this time Lieutenant P and I were keeping watch together and it seems to have been taken for granted by everyone that it would be the two RNVR officers who never got a full night's sleep. He was correspondence officer and I was signals officer, so between us we dealt with almost all the ship's paperwork, which kept us busy all morning and by midday we were on watch again.

Permanent shortage of sleep sapped one's resilience and made it more difficult to take life's little difficulties in one's stride. I once observed to the captain that if one noted the time of sunrise or sunset one could very quickly work out one's longitude. He replied that he had not heard of that, but if it had been of any significance someone in the RN would have thought of it already. That was probably true, but it was not encouraging. He reprimanded me for being deficient in the essential power-of-command-and-officer-like-qualities, with which I was inclined to agree, but I was rather disconcerted by the ground for his complaint: that I did not keep myself sufficiently aloof from the lower deck. In that respect at least his own conduct was irreproachable. Returning on board once, just before midnight, he made me wake up the wardroom steward since he could scarcely have been expected to pour out his own drink.

We suffered a cruel blow in the loss of our first lieutenant, who had done whatever he could to protect us from the captain's little ways. A French squadron that had been lying immobilized at Alexandria since 1940 now decided to re-enter the war. This implied sending it to the United States for refitting and modernization and No. 1 was appointed its liaison officer. When he came to pay us a farewell visit, towards the end of June, he was a changed man, but what delighted him was bad news for us. We escorted the French squadron as far as Port Said and as we turned back for Alexandria he sent us a final message, wishing us luck and concluding, 'Hope things improve soon'. With his departure, there was no reason to assume that they would. One of the disadvantages of the navy, when compared with the other services, is that you can never get away from it, to go for a walk, or merely to spend an hour or two on your own. During one spell of three weeks I was ashore for a total of three hours. When on board, we lived on top of each other and I eventually got into the habit of leaving the wardroom whenever the captain came in.

What with one thing and another, I should have been heading for a clinical depression if I had known what that was. I went down with influenza and a succession of colds. I began to suffer from eye strain when trying to keep station on moonless nights, and to become sleepy on watch, something that had never happened to me before. The doctor offered to do whatever he could to get me a transfer. Things got so bad that I once decided to stop eating, in order to precipitate some sort of a crisis. I forget why I restarted but it certainly wasn't because I felt hungry.

Our flotilla was administered from a destroyer in Alexandria, where Authority was represented by an RNVR lieutenant. Like most of the pusser breed, our captain lived in permanent fear of offending the Powers that Be and their representatives – even RNVR lieutenants – and when we were called to order for being late in submitting our complement returns or jeopardizing allied hopes of victory in similar ways, he would despatch Lieutenant P or me to beg for pardon. We, in our turn, would ask the RNVR lieutenant if no one had told him that there was a war on, and we got on very well. One day, without a word to each other, the three RNVR officers asked him how we could possibly get off our wretched ship. At one time, there were only two members of the wardroom who were not trying to do the same thing. He told me that my only possible means of escape was to volunteer to serve as liaison officer in one of the allied ships, and I replied that I would volunteer for anything.

'French or Greek?'

'Make it French. I can't speak it or understand it but I did a couple of years at school and I'll eventually pick it up. I'll never learn Greek.'

Even if my reasons were somewhat negative, it was a wise choice. A year or so later, when the Greek crews mutinied, for reasons of domestic politics, they threw their liaison officers overboard as well, something that the liaison community regarded as a clear breach of the Geneva Convention. I was given to understand that I could expect to be transferred to *La Moqueuse* almost at once, but I had been in the navy long enough not to count on that.

Partly as a result of No. I's departure, there was something of a Cabinet reshuffle. Lieutenant P and I exchanged jobs, which entitled me to the relative privacy of the ship's office. Experience as correspondence officer would also be useful if I ever pulled off the liaison job. I was also appointed fighter control officer. The captain explained to me that, in the presence of enemy aircraft, he would give the orders, but that I could look after the routine business of maintaining contact with our fighter escort when nothing was happening. In order to discharge these onerous responsibilities I would have to go on a course. This turned out to be rather shorter than my torpedo training course at Roedean, amounting to an hour's pleasant, but totally useless chat at a local RAF station. It was, however, enough to prevent Lieutenant P and me from taking advantage of a boiler clean to spend a couple of days in Cairo. The captain seemed very concerned about this project of ours. He explained to me on a subsequent occasion that if we actually did go to Cairo we would be very grateful to him for having tried to dissuade us. I have no idea what he had in mind.

Lieutenant P and I had begun taking advantage of the ship's communication system to organize a Brains Trust, relayed to all the messdecks. That had its moments.

'What would you call a large collection of eggs?'

'A bloody miracle!'

Nevertheless, the crew were inclined to resent our programmes, which prevented them from listening to their own. General apathy had set in at all levels. When we invited questions for our Brains Trust we got no response. Everyone had become robotic. We went through our routines in total indifference as to their outcome. Some of this was the inevitable product of excessive sea time, but the enemy had not given us any trouble for one or two months and the way in which the ship was run had a good deal to do with the general demoralization. Even the captain had become aware of it. He said that it was because the crew were having too easy a time.

Early in July we found ourselves in Port Said again. This time it was crammed with troopships. A landing somewhere was obviously in the offing and extreme secrecy was the order of the day. A signals officer at Navy House told me that he had been given secret operational instructions to take to each of the troopships. This was easier said than done since the envelopes were addressed to the ships by name and the only identifying signs on the vessels themselves were numbers. Very sensibly, he explained his predicament to his Egyptian boatman.

'You tell me.'

'Well... No. 43.'

Not Really What You'd Call a War

'No. 43? *Reina del Pacifico.*'
'No.17.'
'No. 17? *Monarch of Bermuda.*'
The boatman knew every one.

Assault Convoy

How quietly they push the flat sea from them,
Shadows against the night that grow to meet us
And fade back slowly to our zig-zag rhythm,
The silent pattern dim destroyers weave.
The first light greets them friendly, pasteboard ships
Erect in lineless mists of sky and sea.
A low sun lingers on the well-known outlines
That take new beauty from this sombre war-paint;
Familiar names train childhood memories
Of peacetime ports and waving gay departures.

Only at intervals the truth breaks on us
Like cats' paws ruffling these placid waters.
Our future is unreal, a thing to read of
Later, a chapter in a history book.
We cannot see the beaches where the dead
Must fall before this waxing moon is full.
The tracer-vaulted sky, the guns' confusion,
Searchlights and shouted orders, sweaty fumbling
As landing craft are lowered; the holocaust
Grenade and bayonet will build upon those beaches.

We are dead, numbed, atrophied, sunk in the swamps of war.
Each of these thousands is a life entire.
No skilful simile can hide their mere humanity.
Across the narrowing seas our enemies wait,
Each man the centre of his darkening world;
Bound, as we are, by humanity's traces of sorrow
To their anxious women, alone in the menacing night,
Where the rhythm of Europe is lost in their private fear
And El Dorado could not staunch their grief.

We left Port Said with our assault convoy on July 5. Two days later, in the Gulf of Sirte, we and another destroyer turned back, returning to Egypt to pick up a second convoy and we did not reach Syracuse until the 13th. So I can claim to have participated, after a fashion, in the Sicily landing, but I got there three days late. As we approached the coast I counted 72 merchant ships and 44 escorts off the landing beaches and I missed some of them. Syracuse was still quite near the front line and we could hear continuous gunfire from the direction of Augusta, just up the coast. There were frequent air raid warnings, but these seemed to be provoked mainly by Spitfires, which were often the target for 'friendly' fire, although we did not see any of them hit. The occasional bomb fell and we saw a pillar of smoke go up when one of the landing ships was hit, but, so far as we ourselves were concerned, it was business as usual, apart from the unfamiliar presence of battleships, cruisers and an aircraft carrier. We took our convoy into Syracuse and, when it had unloaded with quite extraordinary speed, took it out again a few hours later.

As we were lying at anchor in Syracuse harbour I did contrive to add a little excitement to the situation. Looking out to starboard, I saw a vague object moving quite quickly through the water. I had my doubts about its identity, but, working on the principle of 'better safe than sorry', I yelled 'Periscope bearing green nine-o!' It was, of course, a 'sweep', towed by a minesweeper that I had failed to notice, but at least it showed that I was keeping an alert lookout. That night, as we made our way back towards Egypt, we saw a good many aircraft towing gliders and one or two enemy planes that dropped the odd ineffectual bomb. It was all very confusing and I heard that we brought down one of each.

We were back with another convoy on the 24th, again for only a few hours. On our return to Alexandria we were allowed our overdue boiler clean, which enabled Lieutenant P and me to get to Cairo for a couple of days. It was hotter than Alexandria but less humid and the scorching air had a curiously bracing effect, like that of a frosty morning. We spent our first day exploring the mosques and bazaars. On the

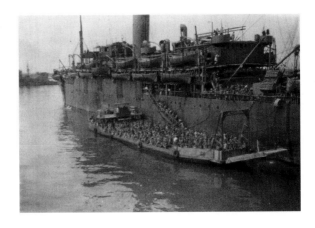

Troops disembarking at Syracuse.

...Cairo...seeing the usual sights.

following day we took a trip to Memphis and Saqqara, seeing the usual sights and we were fascinated by everything: the desert, the scale of the remains and the delicacy of the reliefs in the tombs. We then signed on for a second trip to the Sphinx and the three great pyramids. Despite the captain's dire predictions, we enjoyed every minute and I came back longing for more, even if Luxor and Thebes seemed impossibly remote.

In the meantime the plans for my transfer pursued their uneven course. The captain, who had first seemed well-disposed towards my leaving the ship, had changed his mind and was now trying to prevent it, or so I was told. Early in July I learned that I could expect to join *La Moqueuse* before the end of the month. I went on board and what I saw of the ship and learned about the prevailing spirit within the Free French Navy whetted my appetite. On July 20 my transfer was officially approved, but nothing happened. Then our new first lieutenant fell ill and I was told that I could not be spared for the time being and I was experienced enough to know that the longer a thing took to happen, the less likely it was to happen at all.

On our next trip to Syracuse we took out with us, as a passenger, Commander Gene Markey who, I gathered, was a Hollywood personage of some distinction. He and the captain were the only people allowed ashore. He returned full of enthusiasm for the buildings and the oleanders. The captain's only comment was that it smelled. I enjoyed my long conversations with Commander Markey, for whom I developed a considerable liking and respect, which was not without its influence in developing my feelings about the war. I was still inclined to regard all servicemen, fighting on whatever side, as basically similar unfortunates, caught up in a process for which they could only be said to be responsible in some sort of abstract, unreal way. They might be 'guilty', whatever that meant, but they certainly did not deserve to be exterminated. I suspect that these sentiments reflected a tendency to see the world's proletarians as the universal cannon fodder of their social masters. I was, however, in the process of shifting my ground and was prepared to concede that Nazi propaganda had probably penetrated deep into German society and that, in consequence, the German people *had* become rather different; although I still insisted that there were plenty of potential thugs in Britain who would have responded in the same way. Markey, who struck me as a civilized and humane man, convinced me that what I was beginning to think about the Germans was even more true of the Japanese, who really *were* different and would need to be re-educated after the war. I now wrote home that there would have to be punishment then, but that it should be corrective rather than retributive. In one respect I had not shifted my ground at all: my total rejection of the bombing of civilians. I denounced Churchill for his talk of devastating Japanese cities and accused the BBC of getting hysterical about the inhumanity of German air raids on British cities, while presenting the destruction of German ones as the inevitable price of war. I am inclined to think that that was probably fair comment, but in my attitude towards the combatants I was perhaps as blinkered and inclined to over-simplify as the conventional fire-eating super-patriots.

Once the first lieutenant returned to duty, I reactivated the business of my transfer. On August 12th, in the navy's playful way, I was told that it was probably off – and then instructed to get ready to leave within three or four days. On the morning of the 17th I was hastily put ashore at Alexandria before the ship left with another convoy.

One of the most firmly held beliefs in the navy was that, to volunteer for anything was to tempt Providence. It was therefore with some interest that I waited for destiny to strike. According to what I heard later, the convoy that I just missed was on its way right through the Mediterranean when it was attacked by a German submarine, which eventually surfaced, whereupon it was rammed by my old ship. Until a month or so before that, ramming a submarine had been a court of enquiry offence, since it involved damaging, and perhaps wrecking, one's own ship, but it sounded like the kind of spectacular gesture that would have appealed to the captain. I wondered why he hadn't been able to sink the submarine by gunfire, but I was speculating on the basis of vague rumours. I believe he earned himself another medal. He certainly made a mess of his ship, which was sent to Malta for repairs that took several months. Her crew were discharged and the last I heard of Lieutenant P, until we met again after the war, was that he had been appointed liaison officer on board one of the Italian battleships that joined the allies when Italy changed sides. What all this meant, so far as I was concerned, was that, if I had done nothing, I should still have said goodbye to the captain within a fortnight or so. If I had sailed with that convoy, as I very nearly did, I might have ended up in Malta and never caught another glimpse of *La Moqueuse*. When I think of all the ways in which that would have impoverished my life, I am inclined to wonder, once again, if Providence had not given me its protection.

CHAPTER 6

LEVANTINE MANOEUVRES

T he first problem posed by my new ship was how to find it. Alexandria had no idea where it was, but suggested that I try Port Said. This involved catching the Cairo train and changing en route. I spent the second part of my journey lamenting my folly in not checking that all my registered paraphernalia had changed trains with me, and it was a pleasant surprise to find it waiting on the platform at Port Said. That, however, was not the end of the story. A railway official insisted that my luggage ticket, which was, of course, made out entirely in Arabic, referred not to my collection of suitcases, but to an adjacent crate of small chickens. I had got used to Egyptian inventiveness, but this was going rather too far and he did not get his baksheesh. I found my luggage but there was no trace of my ship.

I spent the night at the Pension Suisse, where I met a pleasant French family, fleeing from the heat of Cairo. This was too good a training opportunity to miss, so I tried to start up a conversation. After an initial period of total incomprehension, we eventually managed to make a little sense of each other, but it looked as though I was going to have rather a problem when I eventually reached my destination. Port Said was no better informed than Alexandria about the elusive *La Moqueuse*, but suggested that she might be in Haifa, so I caught the night train to Palestine. It was crowded but I travelled in comfort since the lieutenant-colonel who had appointed himself officer in charge of our compartment refused to allow any of the other ranks to occupy the vacant seats. About three in the morning when we stopped at Gaza, I woke up, got a hazy impression of moonlight and sand, and began to feel that I was embarking on an adventure. Haifa, of course, knew nothing of *La Moqueuse* but thought that, since she was nowhere else, she must be at Beirut. After a night at the naval base, known locally as HMS *Sandfly*, with the doctor who had managed to escape from my previous ship a week or two before me, I took another train to Beirut, where *La Moqueuse* had just come in for the diesel equivalent of a boiler clean.

That night I was taken out to dinner by the departing liaison officer and some of the French officers. With a unanimity that struck me as a little suspicious, coming

La Moqueuse.

from the representatives of such an individualistic nation, they all ordered frogs' legs. If this was intended as some sort of a test, I was determined to pass it, so I ordered frogs' legs too. They were very tasty, but not exactly what I would have called a substantial meal.

La Moqueuse belonged to a class of ship originally intended to act as fleet minesweepers, but now in service as convoy escorts. She was similar to a corvette but rather bigger and more lightly built and she carried a crew of about eight officers and a hundred men. She had been under construction at Lorient in 1940 when France fell. With the miscellaneous bits and pieces of her second engine piled on deck, she had escaped to England. She was therefore the only ship in the Free French Navy that had been built in France and had always flown the Cross of Lorraine of the FNFL (*Forces Navales Françaises*

The standard of the Free French Navy.

La Moqueuse *had no forecastle.*

Libres). She was also the last of the FNFL ships to remain in service and when she was eventually decommissioned, long after the war, there was a little ceremony on board that was reported in the British press. When I joined her, her main armament consisted of an antique 3" gun that was no stranger to the eastern Mediterranean, where it had served on a British ship during the First World War. She had diesel engines, which gave her no great turn of speed, but an immense cruising range of about 9,500 miles. These diesels had been made in Switzerland. This must have seemed a good idea to someone at the time but in 1943 it posed one or two problems where spare parts were concerned. Two of her sister-ships, the *Commandant Dominé* and the *Commandant Duboc*, were also serving with her in the Levant. The British classified these ships as sloops and sloops were identified by the letter U, followed by the number of the particular ship. Unlike British warships, we did not carry our identifying number on our hull. These French sloops had no raised forecastle and they had a high superstructure amidships, which gave them the silhouette of mammoth submarines. The RAF said that if they saw something our shape, with U 17 painted on its side, they would bomb first and ask questions afterwards.

My accommodation, originally intended for the engineer officer, was in the fore part of the ship, beneath the bridge, so that I would be easily available if the captain wanted me in a hurry. This meant that I lived in close proximity to the French seamen and at the opposite end of the ship from the other officers. My cabin was small but, in comparison with the standards to which I was accustomed, extraordinarily luxurious. I had a real bed rather than a bunk. Just above it was a large drawing board that folded into the side of the cabin and was theoretically secured by a quite inadequate stud. When we hit a particularly solid wave during the night, I tended to sit up with a jerk and the drawing board came down with another, so that we met halfway. I had a desk, a small bookcase, a wardrobe, a (relatively) easy chair and an electric fan all to myself. I even had an en suite bathroom with a water closet and a shower. Instead of having the usual bare steel sides, the ship was panelled. This made it much more homelike, especially for the rats. Even in the steamy heat of the Levant, when the whole ship was like the inside of an oven, for some reason that I never fathomed, the water in my shower always came out ice-cold. Bracing myself for the shock, I had to raise my hands behind my back, as high as I could, and give a vigorous jerk to the very stiff lever that operated the shower. One day I pulled both the lever and the tail of the rat that was perched on it. The surprise was mutual and we departed hastily and in opposite directions. Despite the occasional problem of this kind, I was very fond of that cabin. By the time I had had it painted eau de nil, during a refit, changed the lampshades and curtains and made one or two other improvements, it was just about as unpusser as anything that one could imagine. A visiting Wren officer once said that it reminded her of a student's den, which I took as a high compliment.

Apart from the fact that I was still on a ship, and usually at sea, *everything* about my new situation was so totally transformed that the experience of the previous six

The view just outside my porthole.

months felt like a bad dream. The spirit of that ship's company was quite unlike anything that I had encountered before. Each member of it had chosen to defy the orders of the Vichy government in France in order to keep on fighting. Some of them had escaped from France, others had joined the Free French when they were overseas. Those who had been in the Marine Nationale had been convicted of desertion and their own government regarded them as little better than traitors. This created a fundamental bond between them that took precedence over everything else. Discipline and subordination had to be maintained, but underneath it was the constant awareness of what united officers and men – a mutual respect – which meant that a cheerful ticking-off usually replaced the bell, book and candle approach of the Royal Navy. Most of the officers, I think, came from the merchant navy and the odd ones from the Marine Nationale had rebelled against traditional authority. The result was a general atmosphere of harmony, goodwill and high spirits. They were no plaster saints; everyone had his off days and there were tensions and conflicts of temperament that were inescapable when a hundred men were crammed on top of each other, but for most of the time they were not merely not discontented but positively joyful. They knew that they had made the right choice, at a time when it had seemed a desperate one. By the summer of 1943 it was becoming increasingly clear that they had also backed a winner. This was brought home to me one day when the superb battleship, *Richelieu*, passed through Port Said. She was a beautiful sight, as well as a formidable one, which was more than one could say of our scruffy little sloop, as we waddled out to sea with yet another tiny convoy of ancient tramp steamers – but *Richelieu* had done nothing for the allied cause since 1940. Her only contribution had been of a rather different nature: the *Commandant Duboc* still preserved as a trophy a splinter from a shell that *Richelieu* had fired at her during the allied attempt to take Dakar in 1940. Our crew gathered on deck, proud of their battleship, but seeing her as the embodiment of what everyone dismissed as 'Vichy'. They decided that they were not going to offer any sign of recognition unless *Richelieu*'s crew waved first. One or two of them did, and only then did *La Moqueuse* respond. We might not be much of an asset to the allied war effort but we had our pride.

Once I had come to terms with the language, I felt that I had escaped from an alien world and returned home. My tiny liaison crew reacted in the same way. I overheard one of them, who had been on board for something like four years, explaining to another why he had no intention of applying for a transfer to a British ship, 'You know, Sparks, it would be like leaving home.' When I told the coder that, since he had completed six months' service in a foreign ship, he was entitled, if he wanted, to apply for a British one, he looked at me as though I was not quite sane. We had the same sort of relationship that prevailed amongst the Free French and they dropped in from time to time for long chats. My previous commanding officer would have seen his worst suspicions confirmed.

The wardroom had a good deal in common with the junior common room of my Oxford college. Everyone loved an argument – any argument – for its own sake. The evidence for and against the existence of freewill could keep us going for hours. We also had quite a reputation as a singing wardroom and I eventually acquired … what it would not be quite accurate to describe as a 'respectable' repertoire of miscellaneous songs and sea shanties. My fellow officers had the intellectual curiosity that one expects from undergraduates. The first time that we put into Famagusta there was not an officer to be seen on board, apart from the unfortunate one on duty. Two of them had been to Luxor. One of our first lieutenants had spent a month or two in charge of a shore base in the Lebanon. He used to go for little walks on Sunday mornings and he showed me the collection of about twenty coins and bits of broken jewellery that he had unearthed by poking around with his walking stick.

Although none of our officers had had what he would have regarded as an advanced education, I was amazed, and sometimes chastened, by the breadth of their cultural horizons. One of them confessed to me that he could only cope with simple English poetry – and then went on to discuss Marlowe! When I once happened to mention the medieval poem, *Le Roman de la Rose*, three people began an argument about its authorship. It was now as natural to listen to Beethoven on the radio as it would have been unthinkable in my previous ship. There was nothing high faluting about all this – we could all be as childish as any RN wardroom, and rather more smutty – but we fired on all cylinders. Nothing was taboo and any subject was treated as potentially interesting, or at least worth arguing about. I do not want to draw too idyllic **a** picture. Where France was concerned, the wardroom's attitudes were understandably somewhat ideological. There was a total rejection of everything tarred with the brush of Vichy, and some tendency to look forward to the prospect of vengeance after the liberation. The one opinion that many of them seemed to share with 'Vichy' was that Jews were an alien element within French society. Their attitudes towards people from other countries were inclined to be rather crudely national. The British were accepted as congenial partners, but

Roosevelt's antipathy towards de Gaulle inclined them to reciprocate by a general dislike of all Americans. As we shall see, their contempt for Italians was going to create some problems when Italy became a 'co-belligerent'.

Like me, they were 'bolshie' in the naval sense of being suspicious of all authority, and they also shared my admiration for the military achievements of our Russian ally. On 7 November 1943 the N.O. i/c (Naval Officer in Charge) Beirut asked me why *La Moqueuse* was the only ship in the harbour to be flying a commemorative flag. When I told him that we were celebrating the October Revolution he almost had a fit. From time to time the *Internationale* floated up from the messdecks. The wardroom did not go quite so far as that, but we enjoyed singing a seditious song beginning '*Adieu, chers camarades ...*' that was rigorously forbidden in the Marine Nationale. We also sang our own version of one of the most popular songs of the French Revolution, *Ca ira*, substituting staff officers for the aristocrats whom we proposed to lynch. It was all quite harmless and it was sufficiently in harmony with my own sentiments to make me feel very much at home – until the day when we found ourselves arguing about Napoleon and I suggested that, with all his undoubted merits, he scarcely qualified as a democrat. De Gaulle was accepted unquestioningly as a patriotic leader, on a par with Churchill, but nobody talked about French party politics.

Once I had settled down linguistically, neither I nor any one else seemed to think of me as a foreigner. From my own point of view, I remained 100% British and I was in the process of becoming about 80% French. I lost my British naval identity from the start. Sub-lieutenant Hampson was immediately reincarnated as 'Le BNLO' (British Naval Liaison Officer) to the officers and 'Monsieur le BNLO' to the rest of the crew. This became so much a part of my identity that even now, when I exchange Christmas cards with a former signalman and a telegraphist, both they and I think of me as the BNLO. Our officers changed with surprising frequency – by the time I left the ship I had known over thirty – so that I soon became the longest occupant of the wardroom. Towards the end of the war, when they were arguing about the length of each one's time on board, and I was patronizing them all, I was told that I was excluded from the discussion since I was classified as 'ship's fittings'. We often disagreed but never quarrelled. When we were comparing British and French policies towards something or other, if I preferred the former, I explained to them why they were wrong. If I agreed with them, I would say that the British were, indeed, behaving in a peculiar way, but that in my native Lancashire we tended to see things more sensibly. In the end I think I almost convinced them that the County Palatine was an autonomous principality. They accepted me and I admired them. No one was ever tactful or diplomatic. We all said whatever we felt, confident that it would never weaken our regard for each other. We were, after all, united by a common bond: our detestation of all things pusser, or, as they called it, *fayot*.

My job, like my surroundings, had undergone an extraordinary transformation for the better. This was largely due to both the qualities and the defects of my new commanding officer. Commandant Moreau was a former Marine Nationale officer

Commandant Moreau in command (with the author on his left).

who had escaped from Algeria to join the Free French forces. He was used to having a liaison officer around and sufficiently sure of himself to have no fear of delegating responsibility. His crew hero-worshipped him and he was proud of them. One evening my two 'Christmas card' friends were dining ashore when Moreau came into the restaurant with his current lady-friend. Instead of resenting their presence on such an occasion, he sent a bottle of wine over to their table. This was rather a change from the attitude of my previous captain. For reasons that I never fully understood, Moreau's officers did not share in this general admiration. I think he was perhaps rather conceited and they may have thought him too full of himself and his past exploits. With my recent experience in mind, I was not disposed to be fastidious and he and I got on very well. It was perhaps this estrangement from his other officers that led Moreau to treat me, not merely as signal officer, but almost as his chief of staff. It did not take him long to realize that, if it came to a conflict between *La Moqueuse* and the British naval authorities ashore, I had no doubts about who was 'us' and who was 'them'. Moreau would tell me what he wanted, or rather, invite me to discuss the situation with him. He could afford to give me plenty of rope since he had a quicker tactical brain than I had and he could usually out-think me. Then he left me to get on with the job. The transformation in my position could not have been more complete. I was no longer involved in the day-to-day running of the ship or expected to know about lowering sea boats and things like that. I did not have to keep regular watches and so I was no longer short of sleep. I was free to concentrate on my work as signals and correspondence officer. Since I was not pressed for time, I could be punctilious in responding to whatever demands came from my British bosses ashore, which tended to give them a favourable impression of me. I was under no one's orders but the captain and he treated me with a politeness and consideration that were all the more welcome for being so unfamiliar. I knew more about the British way of handling signals and correspondence than any of the French officers, so, for the first time in my naval career, *I* was the expert. The captain took me to convoy conferences where everyone else was either the captain of something or other or else a shore-based mandarin. From time to time, Moreau used me as his mouthpiece, which gave me a little of the aura of a commanding officer myself. It was I who transmitted his complaint to a lieutenant-commander RN and it was through me that the lieutenant-commander apologized. While it lasted it was lovely.

The little realm of my personal command was somewhat circumscribed. We usually had half a dozen British ratings on board, two telegraphists, two signalmen, a coder and an asdic operator. When I joined the ship they were an exceptionally happy and harmonious group and I have warm recollections of coder Wilson, 'Sparks', the Scotsman who had learned to answer to the name of 'Mackley-Odd' and especially of Jim Woods, who was known to the entire ship's company, from the captain down, as 'Jumbo' and universally regarded as a kind of mascot. The British crew had only one reservation about serving in a French ship: a somewhat defensive attitude towards French cuisine. This was solved by giving them a tiny mess of their own. They got on well with their French opposite numbers and my own relations with them were somewhat in-formal. In theory, any attempt to punish them had to pass from a French officer, through me, to British authorities ashore, and it was simpler not to bother. No one talked much about punishment in *La Moqueuse* in any case.

Life had suddenly become more interesting and enjoyable in all kinds of ways. As I wrote home, 'I feel rather as though I'd woken up … I was thrilled, for the first time in months, by the mere shippiness of being at sea'. *La Moqueuse* could be relied on to give an idiosyncratic flavour to whatever happened to be going on, but there was also something rather surreal about the Levant ports. Beirut was different from pusser ports like Alexandria and Valetta. On the dock wall, just opposite our

Jumbo.

berth, a careful but untutored hand had painted 'The werm terns'. I spent some time puzzling over this cryptic message, and wondering if it could have been referring to me. I heard about a man in Port Said who had provided himself with an identity card inscribed 'The bearer is known to be defeatist and suspected of being an enemy agent. He is to be kept under close observation at all times and on no account allowed in the proximity of naval or military establishments'. He had used this to obtain access to his office in Navy House for the best part of a year before anyone took the trouble to read it. Haifa aspired more to pusserdom, but too ineffectually to be more than a nuisance.

The first thing that I had to do was to get to grips with the language. When I joined the ship, most of the officers spoke fluent English, so they could always explain things to me in my own language. They were so anglicized that they even drank tea for breakfast, but that was a small price to pay for everything that I had gained on other fronts. The captain's knowledge of English was good enough for most purposes, although not infallible. When reproached by N.O. i/c Haifa for being outside the swept channel, he had instructed my predecessor, 'Tell him I'm in the sweep.' They could always tell me anything that it was important for me to know, in English, but I was naturally impatient to become a linguistically paid-up member of the club.

It was not long before I could follow anything said slowly, for my personal benefit. My problem was that, when they were speaking to each other, I could not break up the avalanche of sound into its constituent bits. When confronted by 'NousallonsàBeirutunefoisdeplus', I broke it up in the wrong places. 'Zallonza', I would say to myself, 'I never encountered that in Collins Part I or II. It sounds more Spanish than French, A foideplus must be a technical term for some piece of naval equipment.' There were times when I despaired of getting anywhere at all. Once I had learned how to separate out the different building bricks, so to speak, I discovered that a good deal of what was being said was within my scope. I was soon able to follow a conversation, provided that I was there when it started and was familiar with the subject.

Where speaking was concerned, I was helped by a somewhat cavalier attitude to grammar. In those early days, provided that I could get my message across, I did not much care how outrageously I massacred the language. Laziness played a part too. If you wanted the thing mended, it was quicker to learn the word for tap than to have to say 'You know, you turn the thing with knobs on at the top, like this, and water comes out.' The essential thing was to have done some basic grammar, at however elementary a level. That provided a foundation on which one could go on building indefinitely. Lacking that, my liaison crew, however long they remained on board, never got beyond the sort of basic expressions that we hope will see us through when we go touring in foreign parts. Like pet dogs, they responded to the sound of familiar formulae. When there had been a muster, the crew was always dismissed with 'Demi-tour à droite, droite.' One day, for some peculiar reason, it came out 'Demi-tour à gauche, gauche.' To the general hilarity, all the Frenchmen turned left and the six British ratings turned right, as they always had done. In 1945 I was told that we were to be joined by a British radar petty officer. That posed a nasty problem. If I put a petty officer in the seamen's mess, Nelson would turn in his grave and they would probably mutiny; but if I marooned him amongst the French petty officers he would be liable to commit suicide. I was still worrying about this when he turned up and said how glad he was to find himself on board a French ship, since he had done French for his school certificate and was looking forward to improving his fluency. Unlike those who had done no French at school, he went from strength to strength and was soon able to hold his own in conversation. At one time we found ourselves anchored off the Turkish coast, unable to go ashore and with nothing to do. To pass the time, we played Monopoly for tiny stakes and I can certify from personal experience that there is no better way of learning how to do mental arithmetic in French quickly than trying to work out the rent of Pentonville Road with three houses, before the next player makes his move.

By the end of 1943 I was tolerably proficient, which was just as well. The ship went to Port Said for a major refit, which involved drawing up a vast list of everything that had to be repaired. The work was to be carried out by the Suez Canal Company, whose operating language was French, so that did not seem to pose any difficulties. I was understandably disconcerted when the British authorities asked for a complete translation, presumably to make sure that we did not put in for a gold funnel or something like that. Items like the repair of the wardroom upholstery were fairly straightforward but I have never been an expert on diesel engines, in any language. The engineer officer and I had some interesting conversations, in the course of which I learned that the French for a stuffing box and gland is also the slang expression for a starched collar – a useful piece of information, for which I have yet to find a conversational opening. He would say, with reference to our engines, 'You know, on the top of a diesel cylinder there's a little gadget that goes like this' and waggle his little finger. Even if I had known, that would not have helped very much when it came to describing the situation in lucid prose. People wrestling with the ordinary run of French translation have no idea how simple their problems are when compared to mine. If that text is still in existence, it would win anyone a prize in an anthology of comic prose.

For the first two or three weeks after I arrived on board, *La Moqueuse* carried on with her usual routine, escorting endless tiny convoys between Beirut, Haifa and Port Said. Escorting convoys was familiar enough, but I was now operating at the down-market end of the business, with little groups of heterogeneous escorts and antique merchantmen for whom 7 knots counted as high speed. I was told that if a local shipowner reported the loss of one of his vessels, the first question was always 'Oh yes, how much was it insured for?' Allied sea power in this particular theatre was less than awe-inspiring. One night someone at Port Said reported the presence of smoke at the seaward end of the swept channel. Everyone took it for granted that it must be coming from a ship that had straggled behind its convoy, but it could have signalled the presence of an enemy raider, so all fighting ships were ordered out to sea. *La Moqueuse*, with her single 3" gun, had arrived that afternoon with a convoy. Half her crew were ashore and it would take hours to round them up. All that remained was a small flotilla of minesweeping trawlers. I followed what happened on the radio at Navy House. Some of the trawlers had their crews ashore, others engines that refused to start. One trawler would triumphantly announce that it was proceeding down the channel at 3 knots. This was rashly increased to 5 and then followed by a report that the engines had broken down and a request for a tow. I don't think a single ship had got as far as the end of the channel when the smoke identified itself as friendly.

While we were going quietly about our domestic business in this way, news arrived on September 8 that the Italian government had abandoned the Axis cause and had been recognized as a 'co-belligerent' by Britain and America – but not by de Gaulle, who had not been consulted. We hung signal flags around the wardroom and played the *Marseillaise* and *God Save the King* on our gramophone. We did not foresee that, in one way and another, the consequences of the Italian volte-face were going to regulate our lives for the rest of the year.

On September 9 we received orders to carry out 'Operation Gibbon', which was more easily said than done, since no one had told us what it was. Off Haifa, a motor launch brought out the vital instructions, which were to the effect that, if we encountered any Italian warships that were trying to surrender, we should not discourage them. Moreau, who had been looking forward to something a little more belligerent, signalled to Haifa in a fit of pique, 'The convoy is late as usual', which was true but not very tactful.

Next day we received news of 'Operation Gander' (presumably so designated on the basis of 'What's sauce for the goose' …). These concerned the *Commandant Dominé* but not *La Moqueuse*. For a couple of days the shore authorities kept changing their minds, before they finally decided to bring us in. What was involved calls for a word of explanation about the situation in the Aegean, at least, as it appeared to us at the time. Italy's change of sides had given the allies a brief opportunity to occupy Rhodes, establish an air base there and begin to assert control over the Aegean. The rumour going round the Levant was that, once guaranteed effective protection against air attack, Turkey might come into the war on the allied side. We also heard that the Italian garrison on Rhodes had been open to the highest bidder. The British had sent one motor boat and the Germans a squadron of bombers, which was rather more persuasive. With Rhodes still in enemy hands, the British nevertheless tried to establish bases at Kos and Leros, further up the Aegean. This was optimistic if, as I have read subsequently, the Americans had offered the protection of their long-range fighters for a limited period only, since they did not want to tie up resources that would be needed for a landing in western Europe. This left the British forces trying to hold Leros in an impossible situation. For their supplies and reinforcement they were dependent on light naval forces, which the Germans bombed at leisure as they circumnavigated Rhodes, inflicting very heavy losses. After Leros fell, the war in the Aegean became a cloak and dagger business, con-

There were still caiques around in the eastern Mediterranean.

ducted from small boats by people we thought of as 'commandos'. The situation became rather complicated. When these allied forces 'liberated' a sailing caique, its delighted Greek skipper was liable to go and liberate his friends in neighbouring caiques, for which the technical term was 'piracy'. We took an Admiralty lawyer to Cyprus to try to sort things out.

All but one of the Dodecanese islands, which Italy had annexed from Turkey, and whose population considered itself to be Greek, lay to the west of Rhodes. The exception, about sixty miles east of Rhodes and close to the Turkish coast, was the tiny island of Kastellorizo, not much more than a lump of rock, with one small town clustered round a diminutive harbour. Cyprus is about two hundred miles away, which meant, in 1943, that its Beaufighters could provide a minimum of air cover. I assume that the island had come over to the allied side at the time of the Italian armistice, since its Italian gunners were still in charge of their batteries, under British command. 'Operation Gander' was the order for the consolidation and reinforcement of Kastellorizo.

On September 12 a heterogeneous flotilla set out from Cyprus. In command was the Royal Indian Navy destroyer, *Sutlej*, supported by the *Commandant Dominé* and *La Moqueuse*, the Greek destroyer *Kondouriotis* and a couple of British motor launches. The *Commandant Dominé* soon fell astern with engine trouble and the motor launches had to put into Limassol to refuel. *Kondouriotis*, on the other hand, went on ahead and when we arrived we found her steaming around with all her lights on.

We had no proper chart and there were rocks all over the place, so we nosed our way cautiously into the little harbour, at minimum speed. Close by, on our port beam, we could make out the battlements of a crusader castle, with the tin hat of a sentry moving between the crenellations, which looked like some kind of a sermon on historical continuity. Suddenly the moon rose between the hills ahead of us,

Not Really What You'd Call a War

Kastellorizo, the harbour entrance.

flooding the little town with light. All the houses, the church and the mosque looked a brilliant white, their crumbling defects mercifully concealed in that theatrical light. I heard our paymaster, standing next to me on the bridge, murmur to himself that it was scarcely surprising that the ancient Greeks had produced such poetry, when they lived amongst beauty like this.

Next day we unloaded the supplies that we had brought into the caiques that had come over from Rhodes. This was the beginning of our Italian problems. A fire-eating Corsican officer from *La Moqueuse* boarded one of the caiques and returned in triumph with an Italian flag. Considered as a feat of arms, this did not strike me as particularly heroic. A British army officer came on board, in some distress, and explained to me that the captain of the caique had seen his world turned upside down and was suffering from a kind of identity crisis. All that he had to hang on to was his flag, and now that had been stolen. In the circumstances, the officer refused to leave without the flag. This promised to be a long war. Since there was no one else around, rightly or wrongly, I persuaded the army officer to grab the flag and make off. This did not go down well when our Corsican discovered what had happened, but at least it sorted out our immediate problem.

What happened to the *Dominé*, a week or so later, was rather more serious. That too was all about flags, one of which was stolen, either by the *Dominé*'s crew or by refugees whom she was carrying. According to the story that I heard afterwards, the Italian gunners stood to arms and threatened to open fire on the *Dominé* – and on *La Moqueuse* as well – if the flag was not restored. The Italians apparently sent an envoy with an ultimatum to the British officer in command. While negotiations were in progress, another officer cut the telephone line to the gun battery. This all sounds rather improbably melodramatic, but I am merely putting together the bits and pieces that I heard from one or two British officers. I have no idea how this threat to allied unity was eventually resolved. At the time, we in *La Moqueuse* were happily unaware of the crisis, in which our rôle would have been that of sitting duck. It was rather a relief when British gunners took over the shore defences.

On September 26 we were due to sail from Beirut, escorting *Pola*, a small Italian ferry, carrying reinforcements to Kastellorizo. At 10 a.m. our watchkeeping officers informed Moreau that, whilst they were quite happy to convoy *Pola* and her troops, since de Gaulle had not recognized Italy as a co-belligerent, they refused to do so if she insisted on flying her Italian flag. 'In that case,' said Moreau, you had better get ashore right away since we are leaving in half an hour.' He sent me to inform the N.O. i/c that we might be a few minutes late. I duly reported to Navy House that we had a mutiny on board. I cannot now guarantee the accuracy of my recollection that N.O. i/c left the ground with both feet at the same time. He told me to return at once and when I reached the bridge I found that the captain was already weighing anchor and signalling 'My liaison officer has failed to return' which struck me as a little premature.

We sailed at 10.35 with no officers on board apart from the captain, the paymaster, the engineer and myself. *La Moqueuse* could take little things like that in her stride. Moreau put petty officers in charge of the watches and asked me to hang around the bridge when the most junior of them was on duty. I did this very willingly but quite unnecessarily since he had everything under control. The technical competence of those petty officers left me amazed. When one of them said to me on the following morning that Venus was on the meridian, which meant that a star sight would give us our latitude, I teased him that he was never going to detect a planet in all that blazing sunlight. He set his sextant, passed it on to me and invited me to look at Venus for myself. For an officer who never forgot that he had taken a special navigation course, it was a chastening experience.

We reached Kastellorizo with no problems and this time *La Moqueuse* and *Dominé* were told to anchor outside the port, to prevent a recurrence of our previous difficulties. Back in Beirut, we were given a couple of days in which to find some more officers … and then ordered out to sea an hour later. I forget whether or not we had any watchkeeping officers that time. Our mutineers were imprisoned briefly in Damascus and then packed off to America to commission a new destroyer escort. When we next encountered them in the western Mediterranean, the following year, the incident seemed to have been forgotten. In the FNFL *tout finissait par des chansons*, quite literally, in most cases.

That was the end of the Italian problem, apart from the odd minor incident. I

The *Commandant Dominé and La Moqueuse* at Kastellorizo.

think it was the reason why the liaison officer of the *Commandant Duboc* got his face slapped on the quarter-deck. Nothing in his naval training course had prepared him for that eventuality, but he decided, on reflection, that the appropriate course of action was to slap back, which led to his being transferred to another ship. The crew of the *Pola* asked for their ship to be berthed further away from *La Moqueuse*, whose seamen were making 'provocative signs' at them, and some of our libertymen threw bottles at the crews of two Italian submarines.

To return to our first convoy to Kastellorizo; on the voyage back, one or two of the escorts claimed to have made asdic contact with a submarine. For a few hours *Sutlej, Kondouriotis* and *Dominé* carried out ineffectual depth charge attacks. *La Moqueuse* was not to be left out of something like that. When we made our attack, Moreau called out 'Fire!' but nothing happened. No one released any depth charges and the crew of the 3" gun complained that they could not see any target. We never got a good asdic echo and I was convinced that we were all looking for a non-existent submarine. Eventually *Sutlej* gave the order to abandon the hunt and our little flotilla sailed away, leaving one of its more diminutive elements to stay behind and keep an eye on things. It was almost dark when the submarine surfaced. It sailed away too.

The mayor of Kastellorizo had told me that the island was desperately short of food and asked me if I could do anything to help. The naval people in Beirut told me that I could have anything that I was prepared to sign for, so I loaded up quite a consignment before our next voyage. The problem was how to dispose of it at the other end. A worried army officer told me that it was not the kind of food that Greeks ate, that supplies of more appropriate food were on their way, and so on. In the end I was so frustrated that I let him have my supplies for the British garrison.

On September 20, when we were in Haifa, I suddenly received an order to report how soon I could land my confidential books, which implied that we were being sent to operate in enemy coastal waters. In view of the heavy British losses in the Aegean, that was not encouraging. My confidence in our ability to look after ourselves had not been increased by an anti-aircraft exercise that morning, in which the only thing that we had managed to shoot down was our own wireless aerial. I had more personal reasons for concern: a couple of days earlier I had lost the key to one of the three safes in which we kept the confidential books. I asked a fellow liaison officer, who had received the same signal, what time he had indicated, reported that mine would be ready an hour later, and hoped for the best. Somehow or other I made contact with a local locksmith who came on board to help me solve my problem. When we moved across the harbour to another berth, he understandably thought that we were carrying him off to sea with us and I had some difficulty in keeping his mind on his job. Eventually he confessed that he could not pick the lock, which was some sort of a testimonial to the quality of Admiralty supplies. All that he could do was to knock out the entire lock with a punch. That solved my immediate problem and I got my books ashore on time. Since I did not need three safes in order to accommodate all my books, I was able to leave the ruined one empty. In a British ship, of course, I would never have got away with it. In the fullness of time someone would have required an explanation for safes, defective, one in number, and I should probably have been keel-hauled. I trusted that in the FNFL things would work out differently and I was not disappointed.

What had begun as a romantic adventure, at least so far as we ourselves were concerned, soon turned to tragedy, as the Germans fought back to re-establish their control over the Aegean. We ourselves were never sent into those deadly waters but we were only too conscious of what happened to those who were. When we took men and equipment to Kastellorizo we now brought back survivors from the ships that had been sunk at Leros. After *Dominé* was bombed in the harbour, without being hit, Kastellorizo itself was considered too dangerous. We used to arrive by night and lie up off the Turkish coast by day. The Germans then extended the range of their air attacks to include the approaches to Kastellorizo. On October 29 and 30 two groups of British warships in our vicinity were attacked and we saw a cruiser and a destroyer hit. Presumably the Germans considered *La Moqueuse* not worth bombing unless they were frightened by the sight of our single pom-pom! On the radio we followed the slow agony of Leros, which finally fell on November 17. A week later the officer in command decided to evacuate Kastellorizo in case the Germans retaliated for the kidnapping of their commander in Crete by doing the same thing to him. He moved his collection of motor boats to establish a new base off the Turkish coast, to which we were now directed. I took our own motor boat into Kastellorizo to see if there was anything that we could do. The little town had been badly damaged by German bombing and our attempt to liberate it did not seem to have done the inhabitants much good. A British officer who had picked up a motor cycle invited me to help myself to anything I wanted, since whatever was left would be taken by the Germans. Kastellorizo was crammed with food and military equipment, so I suggested to the officer in charge that we should bring in *La Moqueuse* after dark, load as much as we could and leave before dawn. He thought about it for a while but explained that he would have to make another signal, and declined the offer. I took a few medical stores that I thought might come in useful in the sick bay. I restricted my personal looting to a sheet of Kastellorizo stamps, thinking that if I could convince Stanley Gibbons of their validity, they would certainly have scarcity value. Like all my other plans for effortless self-enrichment, this turned out to be a disappointment.

After that we saw nothing more of Kastellorizo for a couple of months. We went back to our old run, plying to and fro between Beirut, Haifa and Port Said. On December 22 we discovered that we were posthumous since *La Moqueuse* had been sunk at Kastellorizo according to Vichy radio. This was a source of some amusement on board, but if any in France knew that their friends or relatives were on the ship, it would not have seemed very funny to them.

Christmas in Beirut received more than the nodding recognition it had been given in Tobermory. The messdecks streamed with signal bunting and even sported a real Christmas tree with coloured lights. Perhaps the most striking contrast with my previous ship was the endless fraternization between all levels of the naval hierarchy. On Christmas Eve we made continual tours of the messdecks. It was in the tiny liaison mess that I met my Waterloo. I was talking to one member of my little family when another one thrust a tin mug into my hands, saying 'Have some arak, sir.' Without looking, I swallowed the lot before I realized that the mug had been half-full and that its contents were neat. Arak was the local equivalent of Ouzo or Pernod, but considerably more lethal. Fortunately my cabin was just above that mess deck and I had time to reach my bed before I went out like a light, for a couple of hours. I re-surfaced and made my way to the wardroom. I was somewhat the worse for wear but my French was doing splendidly. They told me next day that I had given them an eloquent lecture on the merits of my liaison crew. *In vino veritas.* About 3.30, in seaman's uniform, I led a British boarding party on to a nearby trawler, whose halyards we decorated with the 'Not under control' signal and 'Merry Xmas' ('Christmas' would have needed too many flags). When a sleepy watchman finally emerged to find out what was going on, we retreated to our boat, unfortunately leaving Jumbo behind. He remembered the watchman saying 'I'm on your side, mate' before he fell overboard and swam back to *La Moqueuse*.

On Christmas Day each member of the ship's company was given a small present. The petty officers then entertained the officers to luncheon. In the evening my liaison crew gathered in my cabin and we gossiped until three in the morning, inter-

The liaison crew goes on a weeks' leave.

rupted from time to time by French seamen who dropped in to wish us a merry Christmas. We sailed on Boxing Day to begin a major refit at Port Said. The New Year celebrations were perhaps something of an anti-climax after Christmas but we made up in goodwill for what was lacking in originality. I organized another boarding party and my liaison team took me rather more seriously than I intended and expressed some alarm when I suggested launching a small minesweeper that was hauled up on a slipway.

My main job, where the refit was concerned, had been to translate that monumental defect list. All that remained was for me to keep in contact with a bewildering assortment of British officers, to ensure that everything was going according to plan. I obtained local leave for my liaison crew, to give them a chance to stretch their legs, and then got permission to take ten days off myself. Since joining *La Moqueuse* I had managed to pay brief visits to some of the nearest historical sites – like Sidon and the crusader castle at Athlît, near Haifa – and to spend a couple of days exploring the magnificent ruins at Baalbeck. Famagusta had been a particularly evocative experience since, unlike the other places, it had its links with a European past. Wandering amongst the ruined churches, with their fragments of carved stonework and mural paintings, one could imagine one's self back in England. The cathedral reminded me of Ripon – except for the minaret built on to one of its towers. I did my best to put my feelings into verse.

Not Really What You'd Call a War

Crusader's Tomb, Famagusta

Only the goats' cry and the children calling
In accents Pericles might half construe,
The feel of springing grass and quiet winds
Idling between the mountains and the sea.
A sleepy town that dreams, as old men will,
Myths for its past; these are your comrades now.
Whose life was action, blood and steel on armour.

Impartial rains have carved slow histories
Deeper than tourists, on these weathered stones.
The broken lancets gape like blinded eyes,
The springing arch is down, the column's base
Ends suddenly like sentences half said
And broken vaulting reaches no conclusions.

Frescoes have faded on these crumbling walls
And lizards flicker where an altar stood;
There in the grass the curious eye may trace
Fragments of local stone – the church was poor –
And here, half overgrown, a broken slab
Keeps the firm carving of a simple shield.

Here in this grass the long trail runs to earth,
The silken cord breaks here, and all its course
Through continents and time is fancy's game.
You keep your secrets well; no one shall know
What hills your exile hungered for, what streams
Made music in your dreams, what faces crossed
Your day-defences whilst their keeper slept.
Whether in sun and dust you shared advances,
Did chores here in the base, or helplessly
Heard of the last ports falling one by one.

Whatever part was yours in that doomed play
The set face of despair would be your guest,
Watching the home-bound shipping standing south

Till the sun dipped and gold sails turned to grey,
Knowing for you there would be no returning;
Eastward each victory needing two to hold it,
The core of all your purpose gnawed away
With heresy, and all your rules of thumb
Inadequate, your western certainties
Turned phantom in this enigmatic land.

When the brief winter closed the fighting season,
The undrained land a bog, the roads unsure,
The tall ships chafing at the anchor's pull
When eastern gales assailed the open harbour,
Perhaps in draughty halls the skilful minstrel
Would sing of Arthur, sympathetic smiles
Crossed your unconscious faces, viewless eyes
Turned inwards, grazing country that you knew,
Painting your backcloth to the singer's tale
Of jousting, feasting, women who might still …
And all the wishful dreams that exiles know.

There in the city with your present war
Draining the years away, the tale would be
Dim in the mist of legend, like those hills
Ten leagues to westward, which a sinking sun
Hangs blue against the sky, intangible,
Half real, half imagined. You would see
No mirror in the glass the singer held,
The rainbow bridge of fantasy alone
Spanning from you towards the Table Round.
For us, your life is fairy tale, these stones
The slow grass strangles are another Troy –
Camelot, Famagusta, Manchester –
Ourselves are fact, the last is history,
Time's mist makes legend of the distant third;
Rome, Athens, Troy – the series is the same.
The wake of history spread astern of you,
You played what part seemed best, but now the line
Moves on, to blend your pattern in a whole

Not Really What You'd Call a War

More subtle; as the endless shuttle flies,
Yourself and Lancelot are neighbour threads.

And we, for whom your church by these stern walls,
Silent, before an ever-sounding sea,
Is Chapel Perilous, poised for a while
Above the fog of living, seem to see
Obscurely for a moment, faint as clouds,
Those half-imagined peaks that give our lives
Their fullness and their boundaries. They fade.
We have our work, but turning back we see
A new light on the shipping in the harbour.

Famagusta cathedral.

When I asked the N.O. i/c if it would be possible to get any transport to take me to the ruins of the nearby Greek city of Salamis, he offered me his Rolls Royce. In Salamis I went down into the cellar of a ruined house to examine the remains of the tiny Christian church that had been concealed there when Christianity was still being persecuted by the Roman empire. It contained a – presumably contemporary – fresco commemorating Constantine's conversion. Such historical sightseeing, exciting though it was, had merely whetted my appetite for the Great Event that was now within my reach.

On January 28 1944 I took the train to Cairo. The national museum was closed for the duration of the war so I could only speculate about the treasures concealed on the other side of that wall. I spent a day or two making a more leisurely inspection of the places I had seen on my hasty tour with Lieutenant P, took another trip to Saqqara, broke away from the party and explored some of the tombs that I had not seen before. On January 31 I caught the night train to Luxor. Upper Egypt is memorable enough at any time and season but this was rather exceptional. For the past twelve months I had spent almost all my days and nights on board ship, unable to get ashore for more than the odd day or two, and with nothing to look at but ironware, water and sky. Now I was not merely ashore but out in the country, and what strange exotic country it was. At that time of my life I was liable to be carried away by the sight of any pile of stones, provided that it was a few hundred years old,

The engineer and the doctor at Baalbeck.

Leave in Luxor: the Ramesseum.

Egyptian tourism is not what it was. The author in the saddle.

and here I was, surrounded by some of the most spectacular ruins in the world, with weather like a perfect English summer and six whole days in which to make the most of it. The only thing that surprises me now is that when I went back, over forty years later, it was just as magical.

I began with an excellent two-day tour that took in all the usual sites: Karnak, Luxor, the Valley of the Kings, Deir el Bahri, the Ramesseum, the tombs of the nobles, Medinet Habu and Deir el Medineh. When the rest of the party moved on to Aswan I settled down to enjoy myself on my own at Luxor. The courier who had been with us for the first part of the tour lent me his Baedekker and came to see me each evening to make any necessary arrangements for my next day's programme. I began by making a more leisurely exploration of Karnak. On the following three days I was ferried across the Nile by felucca and met by my steed, a rather lackadaisical donkey whose name seemed to be '151', and his donkey boy. I spent each day wandering on my own, revisiting the sites that I had seen on the tour and adding some embellishments of my own, such as climbing out of the Valley of the Kings and walking over the ridge down to the temple of Deir el Bahri. I also visited one or two places off the customary tourist track, like the temple of Sethi I. Its lonely custodian, starved of both company and baksheesh, gave me an enthusiastic welcome, together with a highly inaccurate tour of his temple. He then made a little speech which I correctly interpreted as an invitation to coffee. Conversation was somewhat difficult since he knew virtually no English, apart from the names of the pharaohs, and my Arabic was limited to things like 'Never mind', 'no good' and various more or less offensive ways of telling people to go away, but we managed.

February 6 saw me on the night train to Cairo, with my head full of marvels and the comfortable knowledge that I was on my way back to something that felt very much like home.

A life on the ocean wave...

... and a home on the rolling deep.

CHAPTER 7

GOING WEST

L a Moqueuse had always enjoyed a good roll. Lightly built, with not much of her below the waterline and quite a high superstructure, she was liable to skid in a strong wind and she kept up a steady pendulum motion, even when the sea looked quite flat. This had its advantages: when you wanted to wash your 'tropical' shirt and shorts, all you had to do was to put them in the washbasin with plenty of soap powder and the ship did the rest. When we emerged from our refit, towards the end of February 1944, our roll verged on the inebriated. This was not very surprising, since we had traded in our antique 3" gun for a 4" and acquired a weighty new radar, perched high above the bridge. I was assured that everything was in order, since a mysterious gentleman in Dakar had a model of our class of ship, on which he tested the effect of new equipment to make sure that we retained enough stability to prevent us from actually rolling over. The 'Old Man of Dakar' was too reminiscent of Edward Lear to inspire me with much confidence and I confess to having had my doubts about him, his model and our seaworthiness. This was an unworthy suspicion: after I had left the ship, at the end of the war, I was told that she had actually recovered from a 55° roll. Her new rhythm was just another of the little ways in which she differed from ordinary ships.

After a week or two of our routine Levant convoys, mid-March saw us back at Kastellorizo, or rather, the floating base off the Turkish coast to which N.O. i/c Kastellorizo had transferred himself. We anchored a mile or so away and I took the motorboat to pay my respects to him. When I looked back *La Moqueuse* had disappeared. During the refit she had been painted in a new camouflage that was quite unlike anything else that I ever encountered. It was said to be the creation of a local artist and it was a kind of Cubist conception, in various shades of fawn. The idea was apparently to make her blend with the coastal scenery when she was on the western desert run, Quite apart from the fact that the fighting in that theatre was long over, it seemed to me a little optimistic to assume that the Germans would play the game and attack her only from the seaward side; but that artist had done a remarkable job, even if it did make us rather conspicuous in the open sea. In a

La Moqueuse after her refit.

landlocked bay the effect was quite extraordinary. I knew exactly where the ship must be, but all that I could see was a fawn triangle that decorated part of our superstructure. Even when I focused on that, it was impossible to make out anything that looked like a ship.

N.O. i/c told me that, when we left to tow a landing craft back to Alexandria, he wanted us to take a German officer and seven men to Egypt. He said that the officer was a thorough Nazi and that it would do him no harm if he got roughed up, but that the other ranks were inoffensive enough. This was rather alarming news. My fellow-officers had told me more than once that, after all that France had suffered under German occupation, there could be no question of our ever taking any German prisoners. I had not worried about this at the time since I could not imagine any situation in which we would be likely to capture anyone, but now we had prisoners thrust upon us. I naturally suppressed the hint about the appropriate treatment for the officer although, when I saw him, I could appreciate N.O. i/c's point of view. I learned from someone that he had volunteered for the army in 1937 when he was still a student and he looked as though he had been created by Hollywood for propaganda purposes. I don't think I have ever seen a more arrogant face, although he may have been over-compensating for the awkward situation in which he found himself. I hoped that he got a chance to see that his custodians were somewhat lacking in Aryan purity. The ship's company included one or two Vietnamese and some delightful New Caledonians who looked like the 'savages' in a children's picture book. The men from the Pacific gave us another advantage over ordinary ships: if we got a rope round our propeller, the captain did not fuss about asking for a diver. He merely sent the New Caledonians overboard with carving knives between their teeth and they had the propeller cleared in a matter of minutes.

We locked up our officer in a small office. After a day or two he complained of boredom. Since he could read French, he was supplied with an exclusive diet of Free French magazines. That was the extent of his ill treatment and I doubt if it constituted a breach of the laws of war. Somewhat later he asked that one of the other prisoners be sent to clean his diminutive quarters. When this was passed on to them they replied that, if he wanted the place cleaning, he could do it himself, which rather raised them in our estimation.

One of the many odd features about *La Moqueuse* was the existence on board of a small cell. I don't suppose that this was much in demand in normal circumstances but it came in handy now. I never saw the cell for myself, but I doubt if it was designed to accommodate seven people. We were delayed for a few days by rough weather which made towing impracticable, and it was very hot, so conditions in that cell must have been rather uncomfortable. The Germans eventually complained and offered to work on deck if they were allowed out of their cell during the day. This was perhaps not in conformity with the laws of war but it worked to the satisfaction of all concerned. A member of my liaison team heard one of the prisoners swear in idiomatic English when he hit his thumb with a hammer, and began talking to him. The German told him that he and the others had been sent to the Aegean since they were regarded as politically unreliable, which sounded very plausible. The French crew offered them cigarettes and every night the sentry who locked them up in their cell wished them goodnight with a cheerful 'Heil Hitler jusqu'à tomorrow morning.'

The next thing that happened was a deputation from the crew to the first lieutenant, arguing that their wine ration was supposed to reward them for the work that they did on board. Since the Germans worked much harder, it was unfair that they should have to make do with water. This failed to move No. 1, but first lieutenants are inclined to be hard people. When we reached Alexandria he was visited again – this time by the Chief Boatswain's Mate who said that, since he came on board, he had never known anyone work so hard as the German prisoners and asking if we could keep them indefinitely. There were limits even to our ability to bend the rules and the first lieutenant turned down that request too, but how could one not lose one's heart to a ship's company like that? If we had been able to keep them, I reckon that it would have been only a matter of weeks before they had been assimilated into the family. There was perhaps something to be said for my belief that the Germans were not a pariah nation and that 'ordinary' Germans were more in need of rescue than of retribution.

One day my British telegraphist presented me with a signal that I had to decode personally since it was marked 'Secret'. This contained an order for my immediate transfer to a fleet destroyer that was currently at Port Said on its way to the Far East. The last two groups of numbers were intended to read 'April fool', but they had been so badly encoded that I was quite unable to make sense of them. The wretches abandoned me to my gloom for a whole morning before they put me out of my misery. I was so relieved to discover the truth that I forgave them on the spot.

We were now almost continually at sea, apart from the short breaks when we were given the diesel equivalent of a 'boiler clean'. As often as not, we did not enter port ourselves, sending one convoy in and picking up another on its way out. Everyone seemed to take this in his stride, although it meant keeping reserves of various currencies since one never knew whether one's next chance of an hour or two ashore would be in Beirut, Haifa or Port Said. Towards the end of April we heard that Moreau had been promoted and would be leaving us. I understood that he would have preferred to remain on board, but was regarded as now too senior for the job. His departure was regretted by everyone as inaugurating a change that was unlikely to be for the better. This was especially true for me, because of the way in which I had been spoiled by Moreau. By now I regarded myself as part of the ship. When, in harbour, I sat around on the quarter deck and watched our enormous tricolour drooping over the stern, I felt that it was my flag, in a way that the White Ensign had never been. My position on board was both familiar and exotic. I had not lost my old national identity but I was in the process of adding a new one to it, of which the tricolour was a worthy emblem. I knew enough about its origins in 1789 to appreciate its universal associations. It symbolised a France of generous hopes and aspirations for all of humanity, a kind of moral community within which I was proud to be accepted as an honorary citizen. Despite all the efforts of the *fayots*, the tricolour has never become a pusser flag. Up to now everyone had accepted me as one of the family, but my situation was less secure than I had come to believe.

Moreau was succeeded by André Ploix, whose character and recent experience gave him a different perspective. In order to reconstruct the situation I have to rely a good deal on my imagination. I have forgotten much of the detail and, in any case, I had to proceed by inference. Ploix changed out of all recognition during the course of the year and I can only speculate about how and why. He had been an 'active service' officer in the Fleet Air Arm and had spent a couple of years in a Vichy gaol before escaping to join the Free French forces. His heart was in the right place but he had no experience of the FNFL – or of ship handling. It took him months to master the little ways of *La Moqueuse*, which were admittedly somewhat capricious. He had missed out on the years of amicable partnership between the British and the Free French forces and I think he probably regarded the presence of a liaison officer on board as a foreign intrusion.

The situation was made more difficult by the fact that the French naval authorities ashore seemed to have been making an effort to assert their control over the French ships on the station. That was understandable enough, but their intervention took the form of requiring their own ships to make regular radio reports when at sea. 'Breaking W/T silence' was regarded by the British naval authorities as one of the more deadly sins, since it betrayed the position of convoys and their escorts. To this extent, both Ploix and I were the victims of a situation that was not of our own making. He had no alternative but to comply with his orders and I felt obliged to report his violation of British practices, which presumably reinforced his conviction that I was some kind of a spy. I was told to stop him and promised the full support of the British shore authorities. If they actually did anything, it was presumably to exert diplomatic pressure on their French opposite numbers, which left me with the responsibility for telling the captain what he was not allowed to do on his own ship. This did not correspond to his view of my function, which was that of a translator, a sort of commissioned coder. Moreau and I would probably have been able to sort things out between ourselves but I did not have the same relationship with Ploix. A year before, I would probably have settled for a situation in which I could keep out of the way and not be responsible for anything, but I had acquired a rather more inflated view of my own importance.

Things came to a head in early July, after we had been out on a gunnery exercise. Pin-point gunnery had never been one of our strong points and on this occasion our performance had been so appalling as almost to defy belief. I mentioned this when I was at Navy House, and was told to submit a written report. Later that day I had an interview with Ploix, when I told him that I had the impression that he had no confidence in me and regarded me merely as a coder. He replied that this was correct and that my only job was to give his signal officer such assistance as he might request. That would have been reasonable enough if the signal officer had had the least idea of British practices, but, under Moreau, that side of the business had been left to me. People told me what they wanted and I had used my knowledge of the ropes and of the people in charge, to try to help them to get it. I was probably nettled by Ploix's comments and I made some rather tactless aspersions about our performance in the gunnery exercise, to which he replied that he would never have permitted one of his French officers to speak to him in such terms, and we parted with our mutual suspicions reinforced.

If my situation with regard to the captain and the nature of my duties had taken a sharp turn for the worse, this had no effect on my relations with the crew and most of the officers. In many respects we had similar grievances, since Ploix began fussing over details in a pusser kind of way that was quite alien to the FNFL. My guess is that, unaccustomed to the local mores and aware that his handling of the ship did not impress his officers, he was perhaps taking refuge in the strict enforcement of official regulations, instead of relying on things working themselves out, as they tended to do. Since this was a reflection of his situation rather than his character, the problem sorted itself out, but the process took rather a long time and its early stages were particularly awkward for me.

It was perhaps to conceal his initial lack of expertise, as much as for their own benefit, that Ploix was in the habit of inviting his officers to take the ship out of harbour. One day in May, before our relationship had become really sour, he startled me by asking if I would care to take *La Moqueuse* out of Famagusta. I was naturally anxious to give everyone a text-book demonstration of elegant ship-handling, but things did not work out quite like that. To get our bows away from the jetty, I began by going astern and pivoting on the springs. The correct practice would then have been to signal to the engine room, 'Stop' followed by 'Half ahead', but in practice nobody played by the rules and they went directly from slow astern to half ahead. So did I. For some reason the engine room interpreted my 'half ahead' as 'half astern' and we began backing at alarming speed in the direction of a trawler moored just astern of us. I managed to sort things out in time, in the approved *Moqueuse* manner, avoiding disaster without attaining anything that might be described as elegance, and we made a somewhat crab-like exit from the harbour. That did not do my vanity any good but it was, after all, the first time that I had handled anything bigger than a dinghy.

For reasons that I have long forgotten, in mid-June, during one of our brief periods in harbour for minor repairs, I spent a night virtually alone on board. The crew had been sent ashore so that the ship could be fumigated as part of the endless war against our rodent population – although we never looked like winning that one. As I settled down for the night I suddenly became aware that, although I was in the habit of using the ship's name as a kind of shorthand for the community of which I was both proud and happy to feel myself a part, without her crew she was merely a collection of bits of iron and steel to which I felt totally indifferent. This was rather curious since the ship, considered solely as a material object, certainly had a personality of her own and we were very conscious of her idiosyncratic ways. Divorced from the people who had made her their home, she might provoke curiosity but she was quite incapable of inspiring affection.

Once our fumigation had started, I managed to get to Damascus. I forget what sort of a lift I organized for the first part of the journey, but I was stranded for a long time at the junction where one road goes off north to Baalbeck. I was eventually picked up and taken into Damascus on a mobile crane, a mode of transport that I can recommend for its visibility rather than its speed. Wandering around Damascus, I ran into two of our officers who offered me a place in their car. On our way back, we cast a regretful look at the signpost that pointed towards Palmyra, but duty called and we did not even turn aside for a quick look at the crusader castle of Krak des Chevaliers, a mile or so from our route. When we eventually got back to Beirut we discovered that fumigation had not even started and we would have had time to look at both of them. Service life was indeed hard!

On July 28 we said goodbye to the Levant and moved westwards to play our inconspicuous part in the allied landings in the south of France a fortnight later. This was the most important operation in which I ever found myself involved, however marginally, and I can remember very little about it and have to rely on the brief notes that I jotted down at the time. So far as the military history of the war is concerned, it presumably ranks as a comparatively minor event, a kind of coda to the landing in Normandy on June 6. For us, accustomed as we were to scuttling to and from with our rag-bag collection of picturesque little escorts and antique merchant ships, the first thing to strike us was the extraordinary scale of the enterprise. As the allied forces began to converge on the French beaches, the whole sea seemed to fill with ships. When we took a convoy to Ajaccio two days after the landing, I noted in my diary, 'I've never seen so small a proportion of water to the ships manoeuvring in it.' And what ships! In the normal course of events, when decoding a signal, if we encountered a word like 'battleship' or 'cruiser' we took it for granted that the telegraphists had blundered, and hunted around for a similar set of numbers that made more sense. It took us quite some time now to realize that they actually meant battleships and cruisers.

My second impression is one of enormous confusion, which is probably a question of perspective. The operation as a whole seems to have gone according to plan and it certainly succeeded, but it probably called for innumerable adjustments and minor rectifications which, when they filtered down to us, looked like major changes. There was certainly plenty of confusion on the beaches. I remember the supreme commander once ordering complete radio silence so that he could try to discover the whereabouts of one of his major units. Faced with the prospect of night attacks by torpedo boats from the nearby Italian ports, the allied ships close inshore were protected by a screen of patrols further out to sea, moving between A and B, B and C etc. That meant that two ships were liable to converge at B. I cannot vouch for the truth of the story I heard, that on one of these occasions an American destroyer flashed a challenge at a torpedo boat. The latter was not very good at recognition signals and took some time to discover and transmit the correct reply.

'You are very lucky,' signalled the destroyer. 'We were just about to open fire.' There was another long pause before the reply came 'You are luckier. Have just missed you with two torpedoes.'

All that was for the future. Our first port of call was Taranto, where we found ourselves in the unfamiliar company of five battleships and two cruisers. What was equally impressive, in a different way, was the fact that the presence of our formidable armada did not deter the mothers of Taranto from taking their children down to the beaches to make the best of the summer weather. My impression that the Italians did not regard this as their war was confirmed by our first lieutenant, who had been at Djibouti in 1940, at the time of the French capitulation. According to his account, both the Italians and the local Vichy representatives were content to stand by while several thousand French volunteers left for British Somaliland, taking eighty tanks with them.

In Taranto we met up with the *Commandant Dominé* and with our old mutineers, who were now manning a destroyer escort, *Le Tunisien*. In our world of coincidences it did not seem particularly strange that the BNLO of the *Tunisien* should turn out to be someone whom I had known at school. We held a farewell party on board *La Moqueuse*, which concluded with a spirited rendering of *Auld Lang Syne* in both English and French. On the following day we made our way westwards past Cape Bon, before turning northward towards the French beaches, as part of a growing assembly of warships, landing craft and transports. We were in it, but not altogether part of it. Ploix had told me that my job was to give our French signal officer such help as he might require, which left the ball in his court. Unfortunately he had completely misunderstood the instructions handed out at the various conferences that we had both attended at Taranto. He therefore switched our radio watch from the frequency that everyone else was using, to one that was not to be employed until D-Day. He then disconnected the radio telephone, to prevent our telegraphists chatting with their opposite numbers in other French ships. His final move was to refuse to hand over the new call signs that had been introduced for the landing. In other words, we received no messages, either in Morse or by radio telegraph, and even if we had been keeping watch on the correct wavelength, we should have had no idea which signals were intended for us. This made life very peaceful for the telegraphists, the coder and me, but I thought it could perhaps lead to an embarrassing situation so I had a word with Ploix, who made the necessary rectifications.

Something similar seems to have happened during the allied landing in Greece. In the rear of the invasion fleet was the large but somewhat ramshackle Free French trawler, *La Reine des Flots*. She too was not in radio contact with any of the other ships. When the minesweepers reported that they had not yet completed their work, the British naval commander ordered an about turn, which was obeyed by all of the ships apart from the *Reine des Flots*, which carried on placidly towards Greece, until she received a visual signal to take station astern of the British cruiser in command. Once the mines had been swept, a second about turn sent the fleet back to the beaches – with the *Reine des Flots* triumphantly leading the way.

On D-Day – August 15 – I noted reports of repeated air attacks, although we did not see any of them ourselves, and of an enemy submarine, believed to be operating in Area Victor. This was all the more disconcerting since we had no idea where that was. For reassurance, we fell back on the BBC, which told us that the landing was going well. On the following day we sighted the French coast, off Cape Camarat, a few miles south of Saint Tropez. By now the sea was covered with ships of every description, converging on the beaches or pushing past us when they had unloaded their cargoes. The only sign of enemy activity was the occasional explosion from an interior that was completely hidden in mist. We left our convoy off the beaches and managed to find the group of escort vessels to which we had been allocated. They were hove to in a circle, a few miles offshore, and everything was so quiet that one of them had actually piped 'Hands to bathe'!

That evening we left for Ajaccio with a score of landing ships. Ploix refused to allow anyone ashore, on the grounds that we knew too much about the military situation, which struck us as somewhat optimistic. From Ajaccio we escorted more landing craft back to the beaches at Cavalaire, where everything seemed to be much more under control, with the merchant ships unloading inshore and naval craft maintaining constant patrols farther out to sea. We heard that American destroyers had sunk a couple of torpedo boats that were trying to break through the

Making smoke.

naval screen, but we were not involved in any action ourselves until the evening. It was then that I failed to obtain my first medal. Since the allies held undisputed air supremacy by day, our orders were to treat all aircraft as friendly until 9 p.m. Just after 9, on August 18th, we heard anti-aircraft fire coming from the direction of Cavalaire. Immediately afterwards we sighted two fighters, a long way off. Each of them was burning a white light in its tail and one of them made half of the recognition signal. *La Moqueuse* opened up with both her twin 4" gun and the pom-pom, but the aircraft were so far away that they probably did not realize that we were firing at them. I was convinced that they were allied fighters, making a belated return to their carrier beyond the horizon, but a motor launch reported having heard an explosion and speculated that a merchant ship had been hit. Ploix ordered 'Make white smoke'. When we lit our smoke-pot there was a brilliant flash of light, followed by a shower of red sparks which lit up the eventual cloud of smoke and perhaps resulted in more reports of an allied ship having been hit. It was rumoured in liaison circles that, whenever a Free French ship fired its guns in anger, the liaison officer was awarded a Croix de Guerre. The circumstances in this case were admittedly rather exceptional, but the anger had been genuine, if misplaced, and it seemed to me that the necessary conditions had been fulfilled. However, it would have been tactless to make a fuss, so I let things be.

On another evening an event occurred that I still find hard to believe, even though I was there when it happened. We were lying at anchor close inshore when a rowing boat put out from the coast with a policeman in it. He climbed on board *La Moqueuse* and asked to see the captain.

'I'm afraid I have some bad news for you, sir.'

'What's that?'

'I have a warrant here for the arrest of one of your officers.'

'Oh dear, what has he done?'

'According to the warrant, sir, he deserted (i.e. escaped from France in order to join the Free French forces) in 1942. Will you allow me to arrest him?'

'No, I don't think I will.'

'I didn't think you would.'

'Well, you've come a long way and it's a very hot day. Do have a drink before you go back.'

I can think of no more spectacular example of the heights of mindless 'efficiency' that French bureaucracy can scale. That Lieutenant X should have been registered somewhere as a deserter is not very surprising. That someone, on this almost uninhabited stretch of the French coast, as it then was, should have been aware of the fact, should have known that the officer he wanted was serving in *La Moqueuse*, and that the particular ship out there was *La Moqueuse* and not one of her almost identical sister-ships, still seems to me almost to defy belief. But what a tribute to a system! Occupations and liberations might come and go, heroes and traitors exchange places, but the files went on for ever. I should very much like to know what they said to the policeman when he reported back. Ploix was far too intelligent a man not to be moving towards the conclusion that, if it came to a choice between *La Moqueuse* and what passed for normality in the France of 1944, there was not much to be said for normality.

For the next month we shuttled to and fro between the French coast and Oran, on our usual escort duty, without any inconvenience from the enemy. On September 2, when we were anchored in a French bay, we were struck by a storm that was quite unlike anything in my experience. There was no wind to begin with, and very little thunder, but almost continual lightning, which seemed to come from every point in the compass. We had a continuous view of the ship anchored nearby, as though we were looking at an ancient silent film. Then the rain fell in sheets, to be followed by hailstones like glass alleys, which made the whole ship rattle. A few hours later we were hit by the Mistral and the temperature plummeted. That was the end of summer. From then onwards the weather got worse and worse. It reminded me of western Scotland and the Western Approaches, except that the 'fetch' – the distance to windward of the nearest land – was far shorter than in the Atlantic. The result of that was that there was much less distance between one wave crest and the next. When heading into the sea, the ship had no time to rise clear of one before it was hit by the next. Instead of bucking, we were battered, almost as though we had lost our buoyancy. On September 19 the weather was so bad that our convoy of landing craft was unable to enter the bay of Saint Tropez. Instead of putting his bows to the sea and going slow ahead, Ploix opted to sail alternately east and west, throughout the night, hoping that he would end up more or less where he began. When dawn eventually broke, we were not merely out of sight of our convoy, but out of sight of land, which was quite an achievement in those waters. We sailed north until we were within sight of the coast, and found ourselves behind enemy lines! We were being observed by a vessel of unknown nationality and if the allied air force found us in that situation, they could have been forgiven for drawing the wrong conclusions. Ploix went westwards at full speed, remarking, 'We don't know where we're going, but we're going there fast.' He might not have fully immersed himself in the *esprit FNFL*, but at least he had acquired the vocabulary.

For the first few weeks we had little contact with the local population. When we sent some food to a couple of local fishermen, we discovered that one of them knew one of our cooks, who came from Saint Tropez, which brought home to us that this was not just another coast but 'home'. Late August found us in the little bay of Bonne Portée where the only building in sight was a large house that was full of plaster casts and copies of *The Studio*. The local FFI (Forces Françaises de l'Intérieur) were using it as their headquarters and we met one or two of them, who failed to impress. They seemed to be living like Boy Scouts, doing nothing in particular and subsisting on food provided by the ships offshore. This may have been a misconception and of course it is not meant to imply any sort of reflection on the French Resistance forces in general, who were taking their full part in the fighting. Rightly or wrongly, we were inclined to regard these youths as '*résistants de la vingt-cinquième heure*', who had only jumped on the bandwagon when it was safe to do so and were in no hurry to jump off. In the general confusion that followed the liberation it was not difficult to invent a flattering identity for one's self and we were too far removed from the action to be able to distinguish the sheep from the goats.

One of the local people whom we entertained on board told me that this part of the coast had been very lightly garrisoned, by people whom he described as 'Caucasians' serving under German officers. He had told four of these Caucasians that, in the event of a landing, if they came to him and surrendered their arms and ammunition, he would take care of them until the allies had established control, and this is what they had done. When I first went to Saint Tropez, the scene was like a Russian film of the October Revolution. Every few minutes ancient lorries, festooned with flags and with riflemen on the running boards, drove off to carry food into the countryside. Rumour had it that the interior was alive with fifth columnists and relics of the German army, who were hoping to defend themselves and perhaps even to counter-attack. We never heard any evidence for this improbable story but it was impossible to get any accurate information about what was actually going on. Much later, when Ploix was trying to send little groups of his crew for their first sight of home in several years, one of his problems was that no one knew what areas had actually been liberated. They were told that if their homes were still in German hands, they should hang around for a few days if liberation seemed imminent, but otherwise return to the ship. Where the progress of the war in general was concerned, we relied on the BBC, but what was happening fifty miles away was a total mystery.

Near Saint Tropez I met a splendid farmer – almost the only Frenchman who has ever mistaken my English accent for the regional accent of a fellow-countryman – who told me about his experience during the night before D-Day. Many of the allied paratroopers had been dropped too soon, some of them in the bay and half a dozen of them on his land. When they had sorted themselves out, their commander asked him the way to Draguignan.

'Draguignan … Draguignan now. I reckon it must be that way.'

'Isn't it just on the other side of that hill? We're supposed to liberate it by dawn.'

'You'll never get to Draguignan by dawn. It must be a good thirty kilometres away. But there's Saint Tropez just over the hill. Wouldn't you like to liberate that instead?'

So they did, which says something about the tactical flexibility of the paratroopers.

The landing in France brought us into closer contact with the Americans, although we did not see much of them as individuals until we moved to Toulon and Marseille. The old antipathy between Roosevelt and de Gaulle inclined the FNFL to view everything American with some suspicion. I think the French population in general got the impression that the American forces tended to see the campaign in the south of France essentially as a necessary step towards the defeat of Germany rather than the liberation of an allied people. Before the landing, everyone had been looking forward to the arrival of the Americans. It was not long before they were treated with less warmth than the handful of British personnel in the area. This was partly a question of scarcity value. The odd Britons were usually involved in some kind of French organization, whereas the Americans had an army of their own. Foreign troops, even liberating ones, are best taken in small doses and there were just too many Americans. I heard a café proprietor say to a customer. 'If an Englishman has a bit too much to drink and starts to make a nuisance of himself, one or two of his friends carry him away. If it's an American, a whole mob of them joins in and they wreck the place.' The British had two formidable aces in the BBC and, less plausibly, the RAF. It was probably quite untrue, but it was the virtually universal belief that the Americans dropped their bombs all over the place whereas the British took considerable risks to avoid endangering civilians. One implausible Toulonnais even told me that when the air raid sirens went off he went out on his balcony to look at the aircraft. If they were British, he stayed on his balcony, since he lived a long way from the docks. If they were American, he made straight for the cellar – but the *Meridionaux* have rather a reputation for that kind of story.

The Americans themselves did not always help. At a time when we ourselves were rather short of food and many of the people ashore were seriously undernourished, we saw the crew of an American landing craft throwing overboard case after case of emergency rations. The tiny liaison mess collected half a dozen, each of which contained 48 tins of meat, biscuits, coffee, etc. When we eventually went to Capri we discovered that American forces were trying to reserve the island for their exclusive use and repelling fishermen who tried to ferry across troops of other nationalities. The mighty *La Moqueuse* was too formidable to be treated with such indignity but they still tried to make our libertymen return on board by 8 p.m. I heard from my old commandant, Moreau, who was now Chief of Staff at Marseille, that the American forces had established a club there for themselves alone. When their allies set up a Franco-British club, the Americans complained of discrimination. Much of this was a matter of luck, the sheer quantity of Americans and their remoteness from their own country, and the fact that the British were often acting in some sort of liaison capacity with the French. It did mean that all things British, for a few years after the war, had a certain prestige value amongst most French people, until the actions of a succession of British governments dissipated French illusions.

At last, on September 21, after six weeks without any proper base, we moved to Toulon, which was to be our home for the rest of the war. This brought us into closer contact with the French civilian population, and also with the Marine Nationale.

Destroying what was left of the quay at Toulon.

CHAPTER 8

THINGS FALL APART

Moving into the western Mediterranean brought us back into the pusser world. On our old Levant station Authority had had a face and the antique merchant ships and their heterogeneous escorts had inhabited a world of their own where the rules tended to be made up as we went along. We now had to adjust to being an insignificant cog in a vast bureaucratic machine whose operations could be as baffling as they were unchallengeable. More specifically, we passed from being under exclusively British control into the hands of the Marine Nationale, which gradually took over responsibility for naval operations in the theatre. Our new superiors were 'North Africans' whom it was difficult to categorize. Apart from a shared language, they had virtually nothing in common with the FNFL, who habitually referred to them as 'Vichy'. This was not strictly true since they had come over to the allied side after the capitulation of Algeria in November 1942. When Darlan said 'Turn' they all turned. In accordance with their training, they had gone on obeying orders when the Free French had put what they saw as patriotism before obedience to their government. The initial choice had not been clear and a good case could be made out for either point of view, but in 1944 the one looked distinctly more heroic than the other. This was perhaps why the Marine Nationale officers whom I happened to meet struck me as a singularly melancholy tribe, whereas I told my parents that life with the FNFL was like being in a mess of Falstaffs. Professional relationships within the reunited French navy were full of anomalies: the officer who had sentenced Ploix to a long period in prison for trying to escape to join the Free French was now a senior official in the French Admiralty. Although the men from the North African fleet had committed themselves to the allied cause, where domestic politics was concerned, they remained true to Pétain's brand of authoritarian conservatism and tended to see the Resistance as a bunch of Bolshevik desperadoes and the FNFL as not much better.

As befitted career officers – in their case it would have seemed particularly ironical to describe them as 'active service' – they shared many of the pusser attitudes of the Royal Navy, such as a tendency to think in terms of form rather than of content, unquestioning obedience to the naval hierarchy and an overriding concern to keep up-to-date with their paperwork. In the case of the Marine Nationale this was compounded by a kind of automatic Anglophobia which contrasted with the easy-going good relations between the Free French and the British forces. I once heard Ploix's successor hold forth on the superiority of the American to the British asdic equipment. He may well have been right but I suspected that he scarcely knew the difference between asdics and radar and was merely reciting his lesson. This Anglophobia seemed to extend through all ranks. When I was taking a stroll in the country near Toulon I met a couple of petty officers from the Marine Nationale coming in the opposite direction. As they approached me they started to hum the *Trente-et-un du mois d'août*, an ancient shanty commemorating the victory of a French over a British frigate, that was part of our extensive repertoire. They stopped when they came up to me and I took over where they left off, which made them look rather self-conscious.

In the final year of the war the officers of the Marine Nationale and the FNFL might have been inhabiting different worlds. I can't remember our entertaining any of them and they certainly never invited us round to any of their ships or dropped in at the Franco-British club. Unfortunately they held the trump cards ashore. With the odd exception of people like Moreau, it was their men who regulated our movements. I don't think it is merely a quirk of selective memory that makes me feel that it was usually the Free French ships that were sent out to escort convoys in appalling weather. I suppose that made sense; after all, they were used to it and the ships of the Marine Nationale were not. In compensation, it was usually the Free French ships that were chosen – I had the impression that this was by the British authorities – for the popular Naples run.

It was not until we were based in Toulon that we could form any general impression of what things were like in our part of liberated France and the most that we could aspire to was a sketchy compound of rumour and conjecture. If there were any national newspapers, we never saw them. The local press, which had emerged with the Liberation, was already flying party political colours, whether those of the relatively moderate *Marseillaise* or the communist *Rouge Midi*. We understood that it was forbidden to take the latter on board 'North African' ships, so, although our officers were not in the habit of reading it themselves, they liked to have a copy sticking conspicuously out of their pockets when making duty calls – which must have reinforced the conviction of the Marine Nationale that we were all Bolsheviks. Both newspapers demanded that the FFI should be given the right to arrest suspected collaborators and called for an intensification of the purge of Vichy officials. Although we were based in southern France, we had no idea of the extent of the summary trials and executions that followed the German evacuation of the southwest, where there were virtually no allied troops. These purges must have offered a fair amount of scope for paying off old scores and pursuing vendettas, but there was no way of preventing them, and an understandable reluctance to condemn them outright. I was told in Nice that the Frenchman responsible for the public execution of suspected Resistance fighters had been shot by the FFI. There can have been few people around who regarded this as a miscarriage of justice provided that the FFI got the right man. In the confusion and excitement of the liberation it was only too easy to get rid of people whom one disliked by accusing them of collaboration, or to reinvent a more appropriate past for one's self.

The town of Toulon presented a curious picture. In its centre were no less than four bureaux of the Resistance, each with a permanent guard of youths with sub-machine guns, doing nothing in particular. Others, similarly armed, seemed to spend their days strolling round the streets. I had the unusual experience of being poked in the ribs, at the cinema, by the tommy gun across the knees of the man sitting next to me, and I wondered if these militants actually took their weapons to bed with them. We were, in fact, living through what student radicals of the 1960s liked to describe as a 'revolutionary situation'. The military display was defended by allegations of the secret presence, in Toulon itself and especially in the hinterland, of German remnants and French fifth columnists waiting for an opportunity to strike back. No one ever produced any evidence of the existence of these shadowy adversaries, but it was impossible to be certain of their non-existence, and inadvisable to advertise one's scepticism. To disparage anything that was related to 'the Resistance' was to leave one's self open to the charge of regretting Vichy.

The reaction of the naval officers was perhaps the only issue on which the Marine Nationale and the FNFL were inclined to share a common perspective. The latter had nothing to fear for themselves. They were, I think, disappointed by the general lack of recognition for all their risks and sacrifices of the previous four years, amongst the exclusive enthusiasm for the Resistance, but they, at least, were in no danger of being accused of collaboration. Their personal security did not make them any less apprehensive about a situation where it was impossible to feel confident of the existence of any forces of order. Nothing actually happened and the peace of Toulon was disturbed neither by the invisible partisans of Vichy nor by the all too visible men from the Resistance. The point was that, if something had gone wrong, there was no one there to stop it. The Communists were suspected of secretly stockpiling arms and the ubiquitous young men with their sub-machine guns did not make very reassuring custodians of the peace. Everyone in uniform seemed to be impatient for de Gaulle to assert his authority and introduce something like regular government.

For a future historian of the French Revolution, it was an illuminating experience. I noted in my diary in September, 'To sit in a café watching these armed civilians, sensing the lack of stability in the present set-up and knowing nothing of what is happening in the interior, gives one a better idea of Paris during the Revolution. All is outwardly normal but one knows that the unseen powers of law and order have ceased to exist. It is so easy to condemn those who, although liberal, shrink from revolutionary disorder, but it's a natural attitude of mind. It would not be pleasant to see the FFI put over its own version of the Terror ... There is no information and no means of telling whether the situation is more or less stable than the personal stories one hears leads one to believe'.

In contrast to all the internal tensions, both in Toulon and in the Midi as a whole, people did not seem greatly concerned about the war itself. I was particularly struck by this when we put in at Nice, which must have been within about twenty-five miles of the front. No one seemed to know where that was and the Niçois made no serious attempt to observe any kind of a blackout. One day I walked out to Eze, a little village a few miles to the east, from which I watched an American destroyer shelling the coast in what seemed a desultory sort of way. To be almost at the receiving end of a naval bombardment was rather an upside-down kind of experience for someone in the navy. Although the front was so near, the only evidence of the war was an American who gave me a lift back to Nice in his jeep.

In between the routine trips to Oran we paid one or two visits to Naples. They gave us the respite of a few days in the relatively calm waters between Corsica and Naples, where the sea always seemed to be much calmer than of the western side of the Straits of Bonifaccio. Naples itself held many attractions. As a general rule, shore-based officers, who disposed of the transport required to take them to interesting places, were inclined to leave their seagoing colleagues to fend for themselves. The people at Naples were much more accommodating. They even provided me with the trucks to take as many of the French crew as chose to go, on a

Away lifeboat's crew!

trip to Pompeii. Every day they reserved a few seats at the San Carlo theatre for the crews that had just arrived from sea. Since tickets were hard to come by, this was a much-valued privilege, which allowed me to see *Madame Butterfly* and *La Traviata*. I got the impression that opera in Naples had something in common with a Spanish bullfight. The atmosphere before the curtain went up was one of fiesta, friends and relatives exchanging news by voice and semaphore across the theatre. During the performance, when the diva pulled off a particularly difficult passage, the opera was suspended while she received applause, congratulations and bouquets. I formed the perhaps unworthy suspicion that, to enter fully into the spirit of the thing, I should have disarmed my British *sang-froid* with a stiff dose of alcohol.

After a day or two at Naples, Ploix used to take the ship over to Capri, to wait for the convoy. When we tied up at the jetty there we found it adorned with a Cross of Lorraine and the name of the *Commandant Dominé*. This was soon joined by the badge of *La Moqueuse*, which was said to represent a French parrot whose out-stretched wings mocked the German eagle. This was spotted by an RAF officer who succeeded in running us down when we were back in Naples. A month before I joined the ship he had been fished out of the water when his own aircraft crashed after shooting down a German plane. Since then he had called each of the aircraft in which he had flown 'La Moqueuse' and worn our badge on every mission. He was fairly comprehensively drunk when he dropped into our wardroom and soon became appreciably more so. All of the officers who had been on board when he was rescued had long since left, but he went around identifying their successors – quite wrongly – as the engineer officer, the navigator and so on, until he came to Ploix, who happened to be there.

'But who the hell are you? I say, who the hell are you? Oh I know: you're the odd bod. Of course, that's it, you're the odd bod.'

I'm not sure that Ploix's command of English stretched as far as 'odd bods', but he entered into the spirit of the thing and the pilot probably got the impression that the old ship had not changed very much. It was perhaps the cumulative effect of our experiences at the hands of the Marine Nationale that was producing a rapid transformation in Ploix's attitude. About the time of the landing he had seemed to me to be evolving in a pusser direction but he now reversed course and embraced the spirit of *La Moqueuse* with quite alarming gusto.

If I am right in thinking that during the autumn the French authorities ashore began taking over responsibility for the Oran convoys, they were still learning their trade. For reasons that no one ever explained to me, our sailing orders always told us to take a convoy from North Africa to Toulon. During the course of the voyage the convoy's destination would then be changed to Marseille. On one voyage in November, when we were senior officer of the escort, no such signal arrived. I sus-pected that it ought to have done, but I could scarcely advise the captain to disre-gard his sailing instructions, on my own authority. The merchant ships duly dropped their anchors amongst the wreckage at Toulon ... and all hell broke loose. Signals had been sent to us: one changing our destination to Marseille and another passing on the interesting information that our convoy was being circled by enemy aircraft. That would have been useful to know since, in accordance with a recent change of policy, the leading ship in each column had switched on its navigation lights, which must have offered the German pilots a pretty spectacle. Marseille had sent Beaufighters out to protect us, while we carried on with our illuminations. According to the story we heard, the delay in extracting the convoy from Toulon and sending it round to Marseille was such that Eisenhower himself wanted to know what was going on. What the situation obviously called for was a scapegoat and RNVR sub-lieutenants might have been designed expressly for that purpose. If they had been able to pin anything on me, I should probably still be languishing in some dungeon, but one signal had been broadcast on the wrong wavelength, another sent out with a new call sign that had never been communicated to us, and so on. I could prove that none of this was my fault and if one of my superiors got his ears boxed, that was not the sort of information that would filter down to me.

On another occasion, we were patrolling off Marseille in the usual atrocious weather when the shore authorities panicked because they had lost contact with *La Moqueuse* – once again they had changed our call sign without letting us know. Somehow or other, without knowing who was at the end of the line, they made contact with us and asked us to try to get through to *La Moqueuse*. So we called ourselves up, using the mysterious new call sign, but, understandably, failed to reply to our own signal, so we told Marseille that we were unable to make contact with XYZ, that is, with ourselves. They must have been quite relieved when we finally put into port.

As usual, we were almost always at sea and the weather was getting worse all the time. *La Moqueuse* and her sister-ships, were lightly built and not designed for such conditions. On two occasions Ploix said that he dared not execute the customary zig-zag but had to keep the ship on the safest course in terms of the weather. During the following month, when we were heading into a nasty sea, a wave smashed a porthole on the port bow and flooded the canteen. This was of concern, both to the crew and to me personally, since my cabin occupied a similar position on the starboard side and when the captain altered course to put the canteen to leeward, it was my turn to get the full impact of the weather. What made the situation particularly serious was that the Marine Nationale refused to allow us any time in harbour for routine maintenance and repairs. On the Levant station, we had had a few days every six weeks or so, but our last 'visite' dated back to the previous June and the shore authorities seemed to expect the ship to carry on indefinitely. The engines – we were fortunate in having two – were increasingly unreliable and one or other had to be stopped from time to time to make running repairs while we were at sea. The capstan was defective so we could not rely on being able to raise the anchor in a hurry. The steering gear was also giving trouble. During one voyage both radar sets were out of action and the wireless transmitter failed, which meant

Anchors aweigh!

that if we got into trouble we should be unable to tell anyone about it. By the end of the year the ship was no longer seaworthy.

Ploix had become as proud of the ship and of her company as any of us, and for the right reasons. He even surpassed us in his refusal to defer to Authority. On our first visit to Marseille we were directed to a berth at some remote jetty that would have made it very difficult for any of us to get back to the city centre. Ploix simply ignored his instructions and made straight for the Vieux Port, which the Germans

113

had tried to block by sinking the *Cap Corse*, a French merchant ship, across the entrance. On that occasion he squeezed by without any trouble and tied up at the bottom of the Cannebière. He was not always so lucky when he repeated the manoeuvre every time we went back to Marseille and on one occasion the *Cap Corse* took off our asdic dome. I was on the bridge and I happened to be looking at the echo-sounder. I must be one of the few people who has seen an echo-sounder register zero. It was Ploix's idea, rather than wait while our convoy loaded up at Naples, to take the ship over to Capri, to give the crew a little excursion. He even sailed her to the Blue Grotto, although the sea was too choppy for us to lower our boats. By now he had realized that he and I were on the same side, waging parallel campaigns against our respective superiors, and that I was emphatically one of 'us' rather than of 'them'. He no longer treated me as a translator but, like Moreau in the days of old, told me what he wanted and left me to get on with obtaining it.

One day in December we found ourselves in Marseille at the same time as the *Commandant Duboc*. We had not seen her since the old Levant days, so the occasion obviously had to be celebrated. That evening her BNLO and I met in the Franco-British club, which was the watering hole of the FNFL. We exchanged gossip until it gradually dawned on us that our two wardrooms must have decided to meet somewhere else, so we took a taxi and set out to find them. I have no idea how we managed it – Marseille is quite a big place – but we eventually ran them down in a restaurant-cum-night club that seemed to have effected the transition from Occupation to Liberation without noticing it. During the meal we were entertained by a young man whose line of patter had failed to keep up with the times. When he reeled off the anti-British jokes that had presumably gone down well with his previous clientèle of collaborators and black marketeers, I began to make volcanic noises, but I was dissuaded from taking any more violent action. When we had finished our meal we naturally began to sing. Scandalised by this breach of etiquette, the small orchestra tried to drown us but soon gave up the hopeless struggle and started to accompany us instead. We concluded the performance with our *pièce de resistance*, the *Marche de Reichoffen*, commemorating a cavalry charge during the Franco-Prussian war, which ended with our bestriding our chairs and galloping round the table. It made a good end to the evening but it was beginning to look like the end of the old days as well.

Marseille: the vieux port.

My old liaison crew had begun to disperse. Derek Smith, our splendid telegraphist, had left us in June and Jumbo followed him towards the end of September, when the French crew gave him a farewell party. The new men tended to be apathetic and to remain apart from the French sailors. We acquired a British leading signalman who took a serious view of his rank and responsibility. He taught his mess all about demarcation disputes and the cultivation of grievances. When we were having a practice Oerlikon shoot, someone invited the British signalmen to join in the fun, and the leading signalman protested to me about his bunting-tossers being required to serve as gunners. To be fair to him, he discharged what he saw as his duty by organising training sessions for the two other British signalmen. That failed to arouse much enthusiasm since, by this time, they were thinking primarily of their demobilization. He presumably regarded friction and discontent within the mess as normal, but it was a far cry from the old days, when they all lived happily together and Jumbo and coder Wilson would drop into my cabin and chat for hours. By this stage of the war I thought that I was prepared for most things, but I had not reckoned on a pusser leading signalman.

The old FNFL crew were disappearing too. When given an order they had been inclined to grumble and to mutter disparaging comments, but they did whatever was necessary. The men who replaced them sprang to attention and saluted smartly but had no idea what to do next. When a succession of FNFL seamen called on me to say goodbye, I began to feel like a survivor myself. We had always changed our officers frequently but the new men had been FNFL people who soon made themselves at home. That began to change too. We acquired a midshipman who had gone through the *École Navale* under Vichy and defended not merely Pétain but Laval. As similar midshipmen joined, I saw them nudge each other surreptitiously during our customary sparring, to see how *l'Anglais* was going to react.

Towards the end of the year we ran into serious first lieutenant trouble. Our old No. 1 had not been the most dynamic of officers – the crew referred to him as 'the Phantom' because he was rarely to be seen by day – but he had been part of the

Oerlikon practice.

outfit. His successor had remained in France throughout the war, serving whatever regime happened to be in power. He was a somewhat obsequious individual who was excessively polite to me and to the British ratings. He even suggested that we should hang a portrait of George VI in the wardroom. To the French crew he presented rather a different face. When he found a messdeck listening to a programme of dance music on the BBC he ordered them to switch it off since he did not want them listening in to British broadcasts. Messdecks and wardroom now discovered a new urge to sing the *Internationale* and portraits of Stalin that were banned on the messdecks reappeared in officers' cabins. Ploix tolerated him for about a fortnight before putting him under arrest – I never discovered on what charge – and getting him dismissed. Once ashore he was said to have told anyone who would listen to him that our wardroom was a nest of gangsters and the captain was in the habit of going down to the messdecks with a red flag and making Communist speeches. When Buisson was appointed our first lieutenant in April he told us that he had been given the sort of preliminary advice that would have been appropriate to a lion-tamer.

The immediate successor to the man who was sent ashore under arrest was a very different kind of person. He claimed to have fought against the Free French during the Syrian campaign of 1941 and said that, when in command of a submarine, he had once tried to torpedo *La Moqueuse*. I found this more picturesque than convincing. I didn't believe that the Vichy forces in the Levant had disposed of any submarines and, if they did, I doubted whether he was senior enough to have commanded one. After that he claimed to have served in the maquis. I have no idea whether or not this was true, but in those days it was not difficult to fabricate an appropriate past for one's self. The new man was of an abrasive disposition, much given to caustic sarcasm. This was too near to the wardroom's tradition of candid comment for me to realize at first that his repeated abuse of the Royal Navy was due, not to anti-pusserdom, but to the instinctive Anglophobia of the Marine Nationale. His discrimination against the British ratings, whom he described as 'foreigners', together with his arrogance, soon made him cordially loathed by all the FNFL members of the crew. When Ploix was away in Scotland during our refit (I never found out what he was doing there) the first lieutenant got rid of as many FNFL ratings as possible. They were naturally anxious for home leave, in order to see their families again after years of absence, and they were entitled, if they wished, at the end of their home leave, to request to return to *La Moqueuse*. No. 1 concealed this from them, with the result that they were drafted elsewhere. When Ploix discovered what was going on, he had the first lieutenant dismissed, but by then the damage had been done.

One night McLeod, the asdic operator, returned on board with his natural pugnacity somewhat primed by alcohol. He seems to have had an encounter with the first lieutenant, which prompted him to mutter something about Vichy. This was unwise if No. 1 had actually served in the Resistance – and even more so if he had not. The first I heard of it was when McLeod burst into my cabin, closely followed

Macleod.

by the first lieutenant, who explained to me in what I can only describe by the untranslatable *voix doucereuse* that he would like me to tell McLeod that he was to go down into our cell like a good boy. I replied that I had no authority to do anything of the kind and that I could do no more than refer the question to my seniors ashore. The business must have created quite a stir since we received a visit from a full four-ringed British captain who came on board to sort things out. He seemed to take a liking to me and offered to get me transferred to a more congenial job. I saw the jaws of pusserdom begin to gape. In desperation I begged him to leave me where I was, assuring him that I would soon get on top of this little problem. Mercifully, he mistook my panic for a steely resolution to see a job through, however distasteful it might be. This seemed to give him an even more favourable opinion of my officer-like qualities and he invited both Ploix and me to have lunch with him. The appointment was for noon and I got there about twenty minutes early. Punctually on the hour, four-rings' head appeared round the door and he asked me where my captain was. When I said that I didn't know, he gave me a fierce and protracted dressing down. I took this philosophically, wondering what was in store for the culprit himself. I had been away from pusserdom for so long that I had forgotten that the pusser conceived of justice as a relationship between officers of equivalent rank. Ploix had only two and a half rings, by British standards, but he was the captain of his ship, which entitled him to special treatment. When he eventually appeared, he was greeted with 'Oh not at all. I was just sorting out one or two things that don't matter. Shall we go and get some lunch?' There was nothing personal about four-rings' treatment of me. He was a charming host and he offered me an excellent cigar. He had been understandably annoyed at being kept waiting, determined to make someone pay for it and, since he could not be rude to a commanding officer, he had taken it out on me. It was quite like old times.

During these final stages of the war in Europe my views on what it was all about continued to show the same mixture of dogma and good intentions, with an occasional ray of common sense trying to penetrate the ideological fog. I still tended to see the war as a conflict between 'fascism' on the one hand and a rather messy combination of conservatism and socialism on the other. Part of my problem arose from the belief that fascism was a degenerate form of 'capitalism', which was there-fore suspect and should not be allowed to form part of any new social order. In the second place, all national societies were divided between 'ordinary' people, who were fundamentally decent human beings, largely unaware of the extent to which they were being manipulated, and those who pulled the strings. The latter were either arch-villains, like Hitler and Goebbels, or well-meaning people who were 'so-cialist' in the sense that they aspired to create a civilized order for the ordinary people. I was therefore indignant when Churchill proclaimed that this was not an ideological war and went out of his way to conciliate Franco, who occupied one of the most prominent positions in my fascist chamber of horrors. I was – I still think rightly – shocked by the trailer to an American film which invited the audience to 'See Tokyo bombed before your eyes', writing home that such a comment would have been unthinkable at the beginning of the war. I continued to condemn any bombing of cities, on the ground that even the most fire-eating chauvinist could scarcely accuse babies of sharing in war guilt.

I was becoming convinced, however, that 'ordinary' Germans were not merely the helpless victims of a bunch of fascist thugs. I was deeply impressed by a book – *Les Allemands en France* – which convinced me that racism was not something foisted on the Germans by the Nazis, but had a much longer pedigree. Claiming to distance myself from what I called the 'ideological Left', I now argued that it was not enough to rescue the German people from the monsters who had enslaved them. A 'generous' peace might merely give Germany a third opportunity to bid for Euro-pean hegemony. What Germany needed was a long period of re-education. The question of her future frontiers was of secondary importance; what mattered was to establish civilized living conditions for ordinary people all over the world. I was now prepared to concede that 'Goebbels' poison has corrupted far more people than I thought', but this did not make them guilty. I wrote home, 'If I had been born in Germany in 1922 what would I have been now? How far is the ordinary German a cause of the trouble and how far a victim?' I was therefore in favour of the execution of men like Hitler, Goering, Goebbels and Himmler, but not of punishing the rank and file, even when they had carried out atrocities. I still thought of these as iso-lated acts of violence. I was aware, in a vague sort of way, of the Nazi policy of depopulating much of eastern Europe in pursuit of *Lebensraum*, but not of their attempt to exterminate the entire Jewish people. That might have led me to revise my views about treating the German population as a whole as the helpless victims of their Nazi oppressors.

Russia posed even more problems. I had always deplored Stalin's lack of con-cern for individual liberty and I was becoming increasingly hostile to his determina-tion to dominate eastern Europe. But Russia was, after all, in some sense 'socialist' and that could cover a multitude of sins and justify a good deal of special pleading. Russia's concern about her western frontiers was perhaps an inevitable response to European hostility in the years before the war. I took it for granted that the govern-ment in Moscow would respect the autonomy of the emerging communist movements in eastern Europe. Starting from this premise, I condemned British policy in Poland, Greece and Yugoslavia as continuing the anti-socialist principles of an Establishment that had been more concerned to appease Hitler than to enlist Soviet help in confronting him. I pronounced that, in twenty-five years time, Russia would be the predominant world power because of the profligacy of the American economy. This did not cause me any enthusiasm but I went so far as to prefer the prospect of partnership with Russia to that of becoming an American satellite.

Looking back, I am astounded by my naivety, but inclined to think that it reflected attitudes that were fairly common at the time, when the general public was ignorant about so many things and those who regarded themselves as being on the Left inserted their concern for social issues into the woolliest of ideological frameworks. In one respect at least, my feet approached the ground. As the 1945 election approached, I gradually lost my reservations about the Labour Party. Whatever its shortcomings, it had to be on the 'socialist' side, whereas the Conservative Party stood for an obsolete capitalism that was liable to tip over into a new kind of fascism. I was naturally delighted by the result of the election. The wardroom, amused by my enthusiasm, if not necessarily converted to my point of view, presented me with a fruit tart which had 'Vive Attlee' written on the crust.

But all that is to anticipate. We spent the last Christmas of the war in Algiers. It took the traditional form of a wardroom party followed by tours of the various messdecks, but everything was rather more subdued than it had been the previous year. The new members of the crew sought their fun ashore, so the ship was abandoned to the shrinking FNFL contingent. Perhaps it is the distortion of hindsight which makes me feel that our celebrations were mixed with a good deal of reminiscence and nostalgia. We sailed on Christmas Day, into the usual gale that was waiting for us outside, leaving behind one of the British telegraphists. I asked for him to be sent after us, in an ambiguous signal that prevented the shore authorities from punishing him for missing the ship. As a result he was treated as a normal passenger - except that he was accommodated in a travelling brothel that was being sent to France to comfort the army. I had tried to shield him from justified punishment but I had not intended that he should actually be rewarded for dereliction of duty. At least he had the grace to express his appreciation.

On December 31 we had arranged a New Year's Eve party when we were suddenly ordered out to sea. It was blowing a Force 9 gale and the 'North African' patrol boat outside the harbour put back into port on account of the weather, even though such small craft were allowed to remain close inshore in heavy seas. It was blowing so hard that we had difficulty in avoiding the cliffs by the entrance to the Vieux Port. At nine o'clock in the evening we heard that a Liberty ship in a convoy escorted by *Duboc* was in difficulties somewhere east of Minorca – we were told later that a tank had broken loose and gone through her side – and we were ordered to her assistance. We set off, away from the protection of the land, and we were soon rolling 45° each way in a very nasty sea. I don't remember being actually scared but I had had too much of this sort of thing and I had to ask the doctor for a tranquilliser. On New Year's Day the port dinghy was smashed once again, which did not matter very much since it would never have survived in such a sea, and part of the guard rail wrenched out to one side. Eventually, without ever having caught sight of a ship, we realized that we must be south of the convoy and turned north, into the weather, to try to catch it up. When we were level with the Balearic Islands it started to snow and a few hours later we ran through a thunderstorm. We picked up a signal from the *Duboc* to the effect that she was making three knots and dared not *reduce* her speed to that of the convoy. It almost sounded as though the rest of them were going astern. As we battered our way northwards, against the most dangerous sea that I ever encountered, things began to break down. The port engine was affected by salt water and the engineer officer got permission to close it down for repairs. It had only been restarted for an hour or two when the starboard engine was swamped and put out of action. If both had been unserviceable at the same time, that would have been the end of us. Our pumps were unreliable and inadequate and we had to fall back on hand pumping to get rid of the water that we were shipping all the time. We lost another asdic dome and once more the side of the canteen on our weather bow buckled and began to leak. We went about, until it could be shored up with heavy timbers, which meant that my cabin had to take the strain. It may have been just my imagination that made me think that it was beginning to give, but it held out until the canteen had been repaired and we resumed our former course. We were pitching so violently that one of the mast stays that was fastened to a bolt on the roof of the captain's cabin pulled up one corner and, since the ship was half under water for much of the time, the cabin was soon awash. It was not until January 3 that we crawled back into Marseille harbour. The *Duboc* had come in the day before, steering by hand. She had pitched so violently that she had begun to break her back and we were not in much better shape. We had also lost about ten feet of our keel when the asdic dome was ripped off. The convoy was still at sea. The French authorities treated us as heroes while the British and Americans accused us of having deserted the convoy. So far as we were concerned, we had never even sighted it, and in that weather – which preserved it from any danger of submarine attack – we would not have been of much use to a ship in distress when it was taking us all our time to remain afloat ourselves.

Moreau, who had been away at the time, furiously denounced those he accused of trying to destroy his old ship. That was going rather far, but we suspected that it was no coincidence that the two French warships out in the storm were both from the FNFL. We were now swaddled with an excess of solicitude, promised our long-overdue refit at Toulon immediately, but ordered not to sail until the sea was not merely calm but forecast to remain that way. We did not know it at the time, but, so far as we were concerned, that was the end of our war.

CHAPTER 9

THE END OF THE STORY

The refit at Toulon began in the usual way, with a conference at which the shore authorities tried to pare down our demands as far as they could, but they were too short on seniority to win more than minor victories. There was so much to be done that our repairs took rather a long time, from the middle of January until the end of April. If wardroom gossip could be trusted, Toulon had its own way of doing things and any job there took twice as long as it would have done in Brest. Several years later I was interested to find that this had already been the case in 1793, when the *genius loci* proved itself a match for Jacobin pusserdom. We had no complaints about that; as one Mistral after another disported itself off-shore there was a good deal to be said for being snugly tucked up in the arsenal, (even if the heat was switched off at 8.30 and, in January, the only way to avoid being frozen was to go to bed). We comforted ourselves with the thought that we had earned a break and the war seemed to be getting along quite nicely without our help.

Since there was nothing for me to do, and the French authorities did not expect me to translate our defect list into English, I took advantage of the opportunity to explore Provence, armed with a pre-war copy of the *Guide bleu*. This was admirable where local history was concerned, but it was something of a historical document itself. When I presented myself at what sounded like a suitably modest hotel in Avignon it had been transformed into a police station and the people there were rather disconcerted by someone who was trying to get *in*. Sightseeing in the spring of 1945 was a rather special experience. The side of the road was littered with wrecked military and civilian vehicles and although there were not many other tourists about, the local buses were so packed that some of the passengers and luggage went on the roof. The customary Mistral blew for most of the week and was so violent that it lifted three bicycles off the roof as we were crossing the Rhône. What to do in the evenings was rather a problem. *Mr. Smith Goes to Washington* just about exhausted the resources of the Avignon cinema and there was a limit to the cups of roasted acorn coffee that the constitution could be expected to take. The bus service, however, despite its reliance on producer gas because of the petrol shortage, was probably at least as good as it is now and I was able to get to Orange, Nîmes and Arles without any difficulty, although I could not manage the Pont du Gard.

In Arles I was more or less adopted by the owner of an antique shop who was something of an Esperanto fanatic. He insisted on inviting me to lunch and dinner – I had brought one or two tins of corned beef with me, so I was able to supplement his rations. He told me that, since he understood German and had had quite a few German customers, he had been able to provide the local Resistance with some interesting information. As part of his campaign to convert me to Esperanto, he had the rather annoying habit of challenging me to name the streets one would have to take to get from Trafalgar Square to Paddington and a number of similar journeys, and rattling them off himself with tireless enthusiasm. I had not come to Provence in order to brush up my London geography. What I was actually doing was reliving the experience of a French master who had inspired us by his account of his adventures in the area, when he should have been telling us about irregular verbs. He had been especially eloquent on the subject of the village of Les Baux, and an army officer whom I encountered in Arles confirmed that it was, in fact, 'fairylike' – in the kind of lugubrious voice that would have been appropriate to a description of the Wigan gas works. By this time the Mistral had dropped and I spent an enchanted day exploring the area. It was very different in those days, when most of the people one met were more at home in Provençal than in French. When I asked my way of an elderly man, one of his neighbours told me that he did not understand French at all. I fell permanently in love with Arles, even if the revelation of what light could do in Provence inclined me to think of Van Gogh as something of a colour photographer.

I took another week off in April, staying at the Hotel Montana in Cannes, which had been taken over for the use of British officers, who were charged 2/6 (12½p) a night for bed and breakfast. I was eventually to stay twice at the Montana and the contrast in the company was rather striking. On the first occasion my fellow guests came from the eighth army. Despite the fact that we had virtually nothing in common in the way of shared experience, we did have a common language, both literally and figuratively, and I soon felt very much at home. On my second visit I was surrounded by people from the first army, who had come down from the north. They were friendly enough, but in a well-behaved kind of way and there was something rather precise and correct about them which made for formality. Living in the eastern Mediterranean seemed to have done something to people. In Cannes at least there was no problem about what to do in the evenings. The RAF officer in charge had managed to make contact with several lively and intelligent local girls who offered me a welcome change from exclusively masculine and naval company. It was also good for my French to talk about something other than defective capstans and frayed signal halyards.

From my base in Cannes I radiated outwards to places like Fréjus and took what should have been some interesting photographs. When I handed them in to be developed at Toulon I was told that they would be ready on the following day. I knew what that meant so I called in again a week later, only to be told that I had come too soon. On my next visit the shop assistant told me that the boy who was taking them to the 'laboratory' had dropped them. That would not have mattered if they had not fallen on some tram lines. That was harmless enough in itself, but unfortunately a tram was coming ... What had actually happened it was, of course, impossible to discover. Some aspects of life in Toulon were more entertaining in retrospect. When I explored the local countryside on foot I was conspicuous in my British uniform and people took it for granted that I would not understand what they were saying about me. I heard one elderly lady say to another, on looking at my gas mask case, that it was ridiculous to insist on our carrying things like that when the war was virtually over. I did not ask her where else I could have put my sandwiches.

Towards the end of April we moved to Gibraltar to complete our refit. During the voyage Ploix invited me to dine with him in his cabin and we had the last of our disagreements. This one was entirely amicable. Remembering my feelings when I had spent a night on board the deserted ship, I argued that the essential thing about *La Moqueuse* was the character of her crew. He insisted that it was the character of the ship that shaped those who sailed in her. There was perhaps something to be said for each point of view, but I am inclined to think now that the weight of the evidence was on his side. *La Moqueuse* had certainly transformed him and I thought of the midshipman who had joined us, hot – or rather cool – from the École Navale, full of pusserdom and high seriousness. Within a few months he had become as mad as the rest of us.

Gibraltar was somewhat changed from the embattled outpost that I had known in 1941. The dockyard was full of Wrens and the wives of the shopkeepers had rejoined their husbands. Nevertheless I started to get the impression that I was beginning a final recapitulation of my years in the navy. We occupied the same berth that *Carnation* had used four years previously and found ourselves amongst the troopships that I had once escorted to Sicily, such as the *Monarch of Bermuda* and the *Johan van Oldenbarneveldt*. I recognized a girl who was still serving in a fruit shop. One thing certainly had changed: the attitude of the Spanish authorities down the road. The mayor of San Roque, overdoing things in his enthusiasm, had put up a war memorial with an inscription in honour of Franco, Hitler and Mussolini, which he was now busy amending; and Franco was having second thoughts about the degeneracy of democratic governments, at least where other countries were concerned. Some of us took a day off to visit Algeciras and I still have the identity card specifying that I was an officer in the French merchant navy. The Spanish authorities probably had their doubts about that, since there were no French merchant ships in Gibraltar, but this was not the time for them to make difficulties.

Gibraltar was an excellent place in which to spend VE Day. Quite coincidentally, I had arranged a party for that evening. The Wren officers whom I had invited would probably have preferred to celebrate in British company, but their presence that night did no harm to my reputation on board. All work in the dockyard had stopped at midday and there were effigies of Hitler hanging from many of the yardarms. *La Moqueuse* hoisted her own, although I suspected that, if we had captured him, we would have set him to scrub the paintwork and argued about whether or not he was entitled to a wine ration. When darkness fell all the ships in the harbour were lit up and *La Moqueuse* hoisted a Cross of Lorraine in red lights; all the ships except one. The commanding officer of the cruiser *Cleopatra* perhaps disapproved of the prevailing frivolity, or he may have been apprehensive about making himself a target for a Japanese bombing attack. His ship remained totally blacked out until the general atmosphere seems to have got the better of some members of the crew and timid lights appeared here and there. At ten o'clock all hell broke loose: ships fired their guns, signalmen flashed V signs, sirens blasted away and tracer bullets provided a curtain-raiser for the fireworks that concluded the show. We heard next day that one of the cruisers in the harbour – presumably not the *Cleopatra* – had loosed off a few rounds into Spain for old times' sake, but that I am inclined to disbelieve. A day or two later a couple of German submarines added the final Hornblower touch by entering the harbour with their German flags flying below white ensigns. 'She's struck!'

Feu d'Artifice

Once more the slow tracer is pinning its sinister roses
Like an evil tiara across the night's black hair,
Once more the small flashes of flame, the reports and the silence
Then the winking of shell bursts that mock the inscrutable stars;
Somewhere, far out in the night, inconsolable sirens
Are keening their old lamentations across the water.

Tonight we talk more than we need and our nervous laughter
Is brittle and quick to evade, for this innocent concert
Is the end of an evil too rank to admit of an answer.
We exorcise war with an auto da fé, the sky blazes.

And we think of the poisonous blooms that we plucked in the desert,
The pulse of a ship in a storm, the illusion of purpose,
And those who will not now be there to inherit the promise,
And we know that the cost of those years is too high for atonement.

The war against the Japanese was still going on, but they were not doing anything in the Mediterranean, so hostilities were over, at least for the time being, so far as we were concerned. There were no more convoys, no more allied escort groups and the French now exercised complete control over their own ships, so there was nothing left for me to do. Henceforth I was almost a passenger. Not quite: since we carried a liaison officer we also carried a naval cypher, even though we never got any more signals that required its use. Since we carried a cypher we continued to receive the corrections to it that had been regularly issued throughout the war. Some of these were very important; others less so. My favourite was the instruction to insert hyphens into 'vis à vis' – I hope that, at this distance in time, I am not betraying any naval secrets. Hard-pressed watchkeeping officers had better things to do than to insert hyphens and corrections so most ships' cyphers were inclined to get badly in arrears. So far as I was concerned, this was all that was left for me to do, so I devoted myself to the job with a zeal that was probably unique in the service. It must have kept me hard at work for something like a quarter of an hour a day. Apart from this vital war work, I flattered myself that I was not entirely useless since I had always seen the maintenance of amicable Franco-British relations as an essential part of the job. That had never been much of a problem in *La Moqueuse*, but with the increasing self-assertiveness of the Marine Nationale it was not something that one could take for granted.

Towards the end of May, Franco-British diplomatic relations deteriorated sharply as a result of a crisis in Syria and the Lebanon which produced an outburst of Anglophobia from de Gaulle. We were in no position to learn what was actually going on, but I formed the impression that the French government had imposed somewhat restrictive conditions on the local authorities, who were intent on achieving their full independence. This had led to violent protests. The French government had then landed troops, which the British government had forced it to re-embark. For a time tempers ran high – but not in *La Moqueuse*, where there was general agreement that both governments, behind their high flown declarations of principle, were behaving in the way that governments are inclined to do, and thinking primarily in terms of their traditional vested interests.

The French were trying to preserve their privileged position in the Levant and the British to conciliate Arab opinion in the hope of protecting their oil supplies. So far as we were concerned, that was the sort of thing that governments did. We were sceptical about all of the moral protestations and had no inclination to demonize each other or to interpret a conflict of interests in terms of national incompatibility. Since by this time there were very few FNFL officers left on board, and the newcomers had no experience of serving in a Franco-British partnership, our ability to cope with diplomatic conflicts of this kind seemed to augur well for the future relationship between the two peoples.

Something, perhaps, had been gained, but I was more aware of what we were losing, as the steady erosion of the old FNFL crew diminished all that had once made *La Moqueuse* unique. Ploix himself left early in June. The farewell dinner in his cabin was a most peculiar business. He had invited as his guest the captain of a Marine Nationale destroyer who defended all the policies of the former Vichy government, as Ploix presumably expected that he would. This was too much even for those members of the wardroom who did not belong to the FNFL. Egged on by the captain, they baited his guest until he finally lost his temper and walked out. I imagine that Ploix had contrived this distasteful scene as a diversion from an emotional situation that he knew would be too much for him. He escorted the visiting captain off the ship and returned to his cabin a transformed man. In a broken voice he said to his officers, 'Some of you are new and I scarcely know you. I have tried not to get attached to you and I have failed. Get out or I am going to cry.' He told me afterwards that he had, indeed, cried like a baby. 'Contemporary' quotations, 'remembered' long after the event, are rightly suspect to historians, but the reader can trust this one since I noted it down at the time and Ploix's words were not ones that one was likely to forget.

At one time the wardroom was reduced to a single FNFL officer, Lapicque, until he was joined by Gardin, whose destroyer, *La Combattante*, had been sunk by a mine in the last days of the war. The wardroom then received a new impetus from the arrival of the last of my first lieutenants, Buisson. In 1940 the ship in which he was serving had been on the point of rallying the Free French when a submarine in the port made the defiant signal, famous throughout the FNFL, 'Trahison sur toute la ligne. Je rallie un port britannique pour continuer la lutte'. This was more inspiring than politic since it alerted the shore authorities who intervened to stop any of the other ships from following suit. As Buisson put it, in almost his last words to me, 'Ah BNLO, je n'étais pas FNFL, mais je l'étais presque.' He certainly appreciated the FNFL and shared their contempt for all things pusser. Just before he took over he had come to lunch in the wardroom. That evening some of our officers were sitting in one of the cafés in Toulon when an officer came in who looked vaguely familiar, despite his moustache and black bushy beard. They eventually realized that it was Buisson, who had been clean-shaven at lunchtime. When he got home he had found his wife dismantling a horsehair mattress and the temptation had been too much for him.

Under Buisson's mischievous inspiration, the *Moqueuse* personality evolved in a new direction, which was closer to the Marx Brothers than to the Marine Nationale. This was no real substitute for the old *esprit de corps*, which had combined a sense of fun with an underlying seriousness of patriotic purpose, but the war was almost over, France had been liberated and we felt ourselves to be living in a kind of postscript. There were no more meaningful choices to be made and we had remained true to our principle that *tout finit par des chansons*. On Bastille Day I was writing letters in my cabin when I was hauled out to join a long crocodile of officers and ratings who were chanting 'Bonjour Monsieur le BNLO,' and carried off to the quarter deck where there was a general sing-song, in which each of the officers was required to perform a solo. When we left for our Tunisian cruise, Buisson, who was unwell, was left behind in France. He rejoined us in the little port of Kelibia, bringing with him a baby donkey that two members of the crew had bought because it was being ill-treated by its owner. We already had quite a menagerie on board, including a fierce old rabbit that clouted the messdeck cats every time they went near its food. Julot, our donkey, was understandably shy to begin with, especially since the wardroom kitten used to go for his ankles, but it was not long before he gave the impression of being quite at home. Buisson had a tender heart and a liking for animals but he imposed an absolute ban on the importation of monkeys. It seems that he had once served in a submarine where the ship's monkey had opened the seawater inlet valve, and that appeared to have given him a prejudice against them.

To Buisson's delight, two seamen called Papon and Valade divided the ship's company into rival clans of Paponistes and Valadistes. I forget which was which, but one of them favoured all things earthy, such as plonk and prostitutes; while the other opted for a touch of class – as Buisson put it, 'wine with a label on the bottle, even though you know it's false'. He once encountered Valade, dressed as an Arab and astride the donkey, pretending to hunt Papon with a rifle taken from the ship's armoury. All of this seems to have gone on unobserved by the new captain, who failed to make much of an impact on the ship. He had spent the war in France and was said to have shown a good deal of heroism when storming German gun batteries in 1944. He may well have been a man of personal bravery but he had the pusser dread of incurring the wrath of his superiors ashore by being behind with his paperwork. He was always most polite to me (which was something that I was inclined to suspect, since it involved treating me as a visitor) but he had the Marine Nationale tendency to denigrate all things British. He was probably a good officer of the conventional sort and he must have wondered what he had done to be given a ship like that, but on the whole he kept his pusserdom to himself and left us to carry on in our own peculiar way.

Toward the end of June we sailed to Cannes for various exercises, as part of a little flotilla of escort ships, most of which had not been very conspicuous during the autumn convoys. As we coasted eastwards we went by the invasion beaches that I had last seen packed with shipping at the time of the landing, which reinforced the impression I had formed at Gibraltar, that I was being given a condensed review of my years in the navy. There was something to be said for being under Marine Nationale command: when a bit of a Mistral blew up the senior officer cancelled the exercises and we remained tucked up in port until it was time to go back to Toulon, which gave me a last opportunity to enjoy an evening at the Hotel Montana.

On July 7 we set off for a 'showing the flag' cruise in Tunisian waters. That brought back memories too, of the time when I had been shelled by a German battery during the last days of Rommel's Afrika Corps. It was also the occasion when I missed my second decoration. The Bey of Tunis sailed by us on his return from a visit to France and we duly dressed ship and gave him a twenty-one gun salute, or, to be more precise, a twenty-two gun salute since someone lost count. Moved by this delicate attention, the Bey sent an equerry round next day to distribute medals which were splendid affairs in coloured glass and about the size of small saucers. It occurred to me, years later, when I was invited to a vice-chancellor's *conversazione* at which it was specified that medals were to be worn, that one of these would have struck just the right note of absurdity. Alas, there was none for me, since the equerry told me that British officers were not allowed to accept foreign decorations without the explicit consent of His Majesty the King. I would have been prepared to risk my monarch's wrath but I had to resign myself to the fact that I was not destined for military glory.

For the next six weeks we divided our time between Tunis, Bizerta and the small ports along the Tunisian coast: Kelibia, Sousse, Gabès and Sfax. We called in at the Galita Islands: mere outcrops of rock where the tiny population seemed to subsist entirely on lobster fishing. Our captain decided to treat his entire crew, so I witnessed a hundred kilos of lobster being weighed out as the order for a single meal. We processed slowly from port to port, entertaining and being entertained by the local worthies, both military and civilian, which could mean two formal meals a day. It was very hot; on one day in Tunis, with the Sirocco filling the air with sand from the Sahara, the temperature was said to have reached 52°. In these conditions life on board a small ship could become rather uncomfortable, and we eventually went on strike against our daily mobilization for formal entertaining and the excessive calorie consumption that went with it, and divided ourselves into social watches, which spared some of us for some of the time

We were reminded that the Mediterranean is not entirely tideless. When we got to the bottom of the Gulf of Tunis we discovered that there was a difference of a few feet between high and low water, which meant that when it was time to say goodbye to the officers who had been entertaining us at Gabès, there was no water in the little port and no way of getting back to the ship. Rising to the challenge, the captain handed me his uniform and waded out to the ship's motorboat while the rest of us returned to the officers' mess. The one who put me up for the night, after we had had a few drinks, told me that he was descended from one of the royalist leaders in the Vendée during the French Revolution – I think it was Charette himself – stood to attention and cried 'Vive le Roi!' There didn't seem to be any way of escaping from history. From Gabès we moved on to Jerba Island, the location of Homer's lotus-eaters, where we had more problems with the tide. *La Moqueuse* was moored a couple of miles offshore and when it was time to return to her we all piled into the motorboat, which kept running aground, although it only drew a foot or two of water. It was an absurd situation; there we were, a mile or so out in the open sea, with the prospect of having to get out and wade back to the beach. The captain took control and posted two seamen in the bows to take soundings with their oars. The one on the starboard side did his job conscientiously and kept reporting 40 cms. His colleague to port, either drunk or bored, waved his oar about in a vague sort of way and called 'no bottom'. Not realizing what was going on, the captain kept ordering the helmsman to steer a little to port since he thought he had detected a kind of channel. Somehow or other we got back.

Tunisia reminded me of the Levant, both because of the excessive heat and because of the way in which the same history, of Phoenicia, Rome and Byzantium, was oozing out all over the place. When we visited the little town of Kelibia I saw from the chart that it had been near to the classical settlement of Clypea. Along the beach were many traces of ancient walls, masses of broken pottery and fragments of mosaic pavement. On the hill above, the ruins of a big Arab fort still contained ancient cannons, one or two of which carried the royal monogram 'G.R.', which posed some interesting questions. History never stopped; the fort had recently been used as a German anti-aircraft battery and there were spent cartridges lying about everywhere.

It was at Kelibia that I was almost exposed to a terrible temptation. One of the farmers whom we entertained on board, discovering my passion for all things archaeological, told me that there were Phoenician tombs on his land and offered to send a man along next day to open one of them up and let me have the contents. We were due to sail at 5 a.m. the following morning, so the question of whether or not I should join the ancient profession of tomb-robbers did not arise. I encountered a temptation of a different kind when leaving the Bardo museum at Tunis. Turning a corner, I almost ran into what looked like the dispersal of a meeting of the Women's Institute, with their veils in the stand easy position. All but one dived behind their protective covering like troops in an air raid. The youngest of them, who was very good looking and not unaware of the fact, gave me a provocative grin and proceeded to do a kind of striptease in reverse, and in slow motion.

Towards the end of August we made our way westwards to Algiers and Oran, before setting off back for France. At Algiers we ran into Moreau who came on board for lunch. He and I reminisced at length about the old days and once again I had the feeling that everything was being brought to a close. I wrote home, 'I feel as though I'm living in the last chapter of an extraordinarily long and complicated novel'. By this time I had started to receive mail for a sub-lieutenant Silvant. I sent the first letter back, assuming it to have been wrongly addressed. When more followed I realized that he must be my replacement. This had nothing to do with the fact that the war was obviously coming to an end – we heard of the dropping of the first atomic bomb on August 8 and my reaction was one of horror. It confirmed my conviction that technological 'progress' was racing ahead of man's capacity to cope with it, and left me full of gloomy apprehension about the future. Where my own immediate future was concerned, someone had noted that I had completed my period of two years and six months of foreign service and I was being recalled to the United Kingdom for a new posting. I had been looking forward to this with mixed emotions. Whatever happened to me, the old *La Moqueuse* had almost disappeared. Gardin and Lapicque, our only remaining FNFL officers, together with what was left of the FNFL crew, would soon be leaving and the attitude of the people who were joining us was not particularly congenial. One of our new officers proclaimed his unconditional loyalty to Pétain – who had just been put on trial – and three more approved of Pétain's brand of authoritarian conservatism, although not of his submissive attitude towards Germany. Once the war was over, it could only be a matter of weeks before all liaison officers were withdrawn from French ships, so this chapter of my life was coming to a close. Rather than hang around waiting for my eventual demobilization, my thoughts turned increasingly towards the accelerated 'Class B' release that was being offered to people whose university studies had been interrupted by military service. This had not seemed an irresistible temptation as an alternative to what I had once known as *La Moqueuse*, but since that was in the last stages of dissolution ...

When we returned to Toulon on September 9 sub-lieutenant Silvant presented himself on board. I seem to have suffered a belated attack of pusserdom, or perhaps I was merely reluctant to resign myself to the inevitable. For whatever reason, I decided that I could not leave the ship until I received an explicit order to that effect. A day or two later, without any letter of explanation, I was sent a copy of the latest edition of the Station Movement Orders. Thumbing through it, I eventually discovered that Lieutenant Hampson was transferred from HMS *St. Angelo* (alias Malta) to HMS *Victory*. That looked clear enough but I wanted to do things properly. I knew that no one was allowed to leave a British warship without the authorization of the captain and I was, to all intents and purposes, the captain of the tiny British fraction of *La Moqueuse*, so I wrote a letter to Vice-Admiral Malta, telling him that Lieutenant Hampson had shown me the movement order and that I had given him my permission to leave the ship on September 11. That perhaps looked a little odd, but so did a good many other things in the navy.

This was the end, and not merely for me. Most of the remnants of the FNFL crew left on the 10th, after coming to the wardroom to say goodbye and leaving Buisson almost in tears. Lapicque and Gardin were both leaving for Paris. I was anxious to spend a few days there myself, with one of my companions from the Hotel Montana who had gone back home, and Gardin offered to put me up in the flat that his sister had preserved for the family while its masculine members were hidden away in the south of France, in a German prisoner of war camp, in the FNFL and even the Marine Nationale. Parting from *La Moqueuse* was a sad occasion for us all but the unhappiest man was probably Buisson who was only too well aware of the fact that he was being left to preside over the ruins. The funeral rites went on for days. The wardroom presented me with a pipe and Mme Buisson gave me a book of the sea shanties that we had all sung together. I was loaded with souvenirs: the Free French jack with its Cross of Lorraine that had flown from our bows, and a metal plaque with a rather demure young moqueuse wearing a revolutionary Phrygian bonnet, that hangs in front of me as I am writing this. After dividing up my carefully hoarded stock of whisky between the wardroom, my liaison crew and the petty officers' mess, I took Lapicque with me in the duty car for Marseille, where the rail transport officer gave me a warrant for Manchester. I travelled with Lapicque and of course Moreau was on the same train, to bring everything to an appropriate conclusion. All I remember of the journey to Paris is that it took nineteen hours and that, when I was stretching my legs on the platform at Lyon, a bewildered passenger mistook me for a railway official and started asking me for directions.

I spent a few very enjoyable days in Paris, where I went to see Anouilh's *Antigone*, which seemed so relevant to everyone's recent experiences that I have never known a theatre audience so completely absorbed in a production, which was heard in a strange sort of positive silence. Gardin's sister made me very welcome and we had some most agreeable conversations late into the night, but we did not actually get married until I had taken my degree. This was a time of beginnings as well as endings.

At midnight on the 18th I caught the train to Dieppe and the night ferry. One of the many advantages of being, or having been, a liaison officer was that one slipped through the cogs of the machine and no one seemed very much concerned about one's doings. I could have gone straight home but sooner or later I would have to present myself at the Admiralty, and it seemed simpler to do that when I was passing through London. I was shown into the office of an RNVR lieutenant-commander who was wearing a uniform that looked as though it had just come from Moss Bros. He gave the impression that he had spent the war navigating between the Admiralty and Bond Street. That, of course, is entirely unfair and, for all that I know, he may have served his time on Murmansk convoys, but I had been living – and occasionally sleeping – in my old uniform for the past three years and I had not been able to get a shave on the ferry, so I was feeling at rather a disadvantage.

Two and a half rings hoisted an Admiralty pattern smile.

'What group are you in for demobilization?'

'Forty,' I said grimly. One's group was determined by age and length of service, group one being the best. Those in group forty looked like being pensioned off before they were due for release from the navy.

'Ah yes, forty' he said amiably. 'Tell me, how does the idea of some service abroad appeal to you?'

I can't remember whether or not I told him. This was no time for half measures so I did not bother to point out that I had been doing precisely that for 951 of the previous 951½ days.

'I understand that I am being considered for a Class B release so that I can return to the university.'

Two and a half rings cancelled the smile.

'In that case you had better go and see *Mr* So and So in room XYZ.'

Mr So and So turned out to be a large and genial man in his shirtsleeves.

'Hampson … Hampson? Thought you were in Malta. Made a signal about you a couple of days ago. Yes, here it is. If you like, we'll demobilize you now, but it will take a day or two. If I were you I'd go home and we'll do it by post.'

It was as simple as that. When I left the building I walked out of the navy. Over the previous four years I had felt from time to time that if they managed to give me a military funeral (with seamen from other ships, who had never heard of me, cursing me because they had been made to turn out for my funeral party when they should have been enjoying a make and mend), that would have been the navy's final victory. I had won that one, anyway.

Not Really What You'd Call a War

I sat in the train from Euston, watching the unfamiliar English countryside roll slowly past the window. It had not really been what you'd call a war, but it had given me a wife and a vocation, although I was not aware of either of these things at the time, together with a lifetime's immunization against pusserdom, for all of which I have never stopped being deeply grateful.